How Can You Become the Boss?

How Can You Become the Boss?

From Personal Mastery to Organizational Transformation

Sister Mary Ann Jacobs and
Sister Remigia Kushner

ROWMAN & LITTLEFIELD
Lanham • Boulder • New York • London

Published by Rowman & Littlefield
A wholly owned subsidiary of The Rowman & Littlefield Publishing Group, Inc.
4501 Forbes Boulevard, Suite 200, Lanham, Maryland 20706
www.rowman.com

Unit A, Whitacre Mews, 26–34 Stannary Street, London SE11 4AB

Copyright © 2017 by Mary Ann Jacobs and Remigia Kushner

All rights reserved. No part of this book may be reproduced in any form or by any electronic or mechanical means, including information storage and retrieval systems, without written permission from the publisher, except by a reviewer who may quote passages in a review.

British Library Cataloguing in Publication Information Available

Library of Congress Cataloging-in-Publication Data is Available
ISBN 978-1-4758-3231-0 (cloth: alk. paper)
ISBN 978-1-4758-3232-7 (pbk: alk. paper)
ISBN 978-1-4758-3235-8 (electronic)

∞™ The paper used in this publication meets the minimum requirements of American National Standard for Information Sciences—Permanence of Paper for Printed Library Materials, ANSI/NISO Z39.48–1992.

Printed in the United States of America

Contents

Introduction   vii

PART I: LEADERSHIP DEVELOPMENT   1

1   Lead, Follow, or Get Out of the Way   3
2   Secrets of Leadership   13
3   Growing into Leadership   23

PART II: LEADING SELF   31

4   The Secret of Getting Ahead Is Getting Started   33
5   If You Always Succeed, You Are Overqualified   45
6   All Change Begins with a Change of Mind   59

PART III: LEADING OTHERS TO LEAD THEMSELVES   71

7   Find a Parade and Get in Front of It   73
8   Fusing Power and People   85
9   From Dependence to Independence to Interdependence   97

PART IV: LEADING/TRANSFORMING THE ORGANIZATION	**107**
10 All of Us Is Smarter than One of Us	109
11 If You Want to Be Smart, Hire Up	121
12 A Platform for Spreading Ideas That Work	133
PART V: THE FUTURE OF LEADERSHIP	**145**
13 Leadership Is Action, Not Position	147
14 Whatever You Are, Be a Good One	157
15 Participantship: The Future of Leadership	167
Index	179
Contributors	183

Introduction

Why write another book on leadership when the market is exploding with what leadership is, what it isn't, how to develop leaders, how to fire them, how leaders transform organizations, and how they destroy them? These authors are privileged to teach in a graduate level leadership program and share their own twenty-five plus years of leadership experience, the insights gained from working with others in transforming organizations, and the disasters noted when leadership is not worthy of the name.

Part I points out the characteristics of leadership that will be considered in this book. Each set of characteristics will be treated in separate chapters. Part I will describe the relation of personal mastery to organizational transformation. The components of leadership—mission and vision, using time, developing the will to learn, promoting personal mastery through self-talk, and problem solving—are explained in relation to moving from dependence to independence to interdependence.

Part II deals with the knowledge, skills, and dispositions for leading self. Part III treats relational characteristics with a view to leading others to develop or enhance their own leadership characteristics. Part IV considers the importance of characteristics to the continuous improvement of the organization, the ongoing transformation into more of what the organization is intended to be.

There will be some reflection opportunities to think about personal, relational, and organizational leadership characteristics. At the end of Parts II, III, and IV, reflective questions and challenges will give an opportunity to think about how these topics affect individuals in every walk of life.

Recognizing leadership in action sometimes requires recognizing what happens when real leadership is lacking or missing or the opposite of real leadership is true. Some chapters, then, will tell what happens when those in positions of leadership are not really leaders; instead, they are placeholders in hierarchical positions. Look for the "What if They Don't?" stories about bad leadership in organizations.

This is a necessary consideration because everyone is born into an organization. Everyone lives through organizations, whether as a parent or child, priest or believer, a teacher or student, administrator, a CEO, a chairman of the board, or the president of the company. For better or for worse, leadership is integral to any organization. As history and current events have shown, leadership is not static or fixed, but rather grows and develops, sometimes by the sheer will of the leader, sometimes because of circumstances.

Part V deals with some conjectures about the future of leadership and how leadership may evolve into the future. The future of leadership is more collective, more centered in participantship that produces an authentic, honest, and mission-driven organization.

This book will meet this need by presenting knowledge, skills, and dispositions for leading self, leading others to lead themselves, and leading with others to transform organizations.

Part I

LEADERSHIP DEVELOPMENT

Are leaders born or made? The answer is "yes." Those who are born leaders seem to have everything going for them—presence, charm, talent, *height*, *voice*—social skills and physical attributes. In this book, there will be some caveats about born leaders along with a description of studies. However, when the characteristics of effective or productive leaders are described, it turns out that those characteristics can be imitated and developed in *made leaders*.

Part I presents the journey of becoming a made leader, the norm for most leaders. Some important road signs on the journey include leading self before trying to lead others. When leading self becomes real, the next leg of the journey is to lead others, to lead them to lead themselves, not just to follow the leader. It is more important to become a leader.

The final leg of the journey is to lead with those leaders to transform the organization to fulfill its vision and mission.

LEADERSHIP DEVELOPMENT

Chapter 1

Lead, Follow, or Get Out of the Way

> *The most dangerous leadership myth is that leaders are born—that there is a genetic factor to leadership. This myth asserts that people simply either have certain charismatic qualities or not. That's nonsense; in fact, the opposite is true. Leaders are made rather than born. And the way we become leaders is by learning about leadership through life and job experiences.*
>
> —Warren Bennis

There are many books and studies about leadership—the science of it, the art of it. Mostly, leadership is a mystery. Mother Teresa and Hitler are leaders! In their cases, it is the use of their leadership that makes the difference. But what about leadership in ordinary people, some who hold hierarchical positions and have no leadership skill at all, some who are leaders and have no positions at all? What about the leadership of parents and teachers?

This chapter examines leadership development. If it walks like a duck and quacks like a duck, there is a good chance that it is a duck. A title does not make a leader. In many cases, the title simply describes a position and the responsibilities of the person who holds the position. However, if the characteristics of authentic leadership can be described, then those characteristics can be imitated. This chapter explores the characteristics of leaders.

HISTORY OF LEADERSHIP

Joseph Rost and others, including James MacGregor Burns, Warren Bennis, and Henry Mintzberg, argue that the entire history of modern leadership studies has been seriously flawed. First, while there is much talk about leadership, no one has actually defined what leadership is. The idea of leadership is like art—you know it when you see it.

Second, social scientists have studied leadership from their own fields. Thus, political leadership is regarded through the lens of politics, group psychologists see it as group facilitation, and education and business define it as educational administration or as business management. Leadership is so much more.

Leadership studies of the twentieth century regarded leadership as an art of the elite and leaders as those few people with built-in genius! And then, there are the rest who merely admire the elite. The 1900s saw the inception of the great-man theories. These theories of leadership held that the leader was born great and thus inherited greatness. The belief was that great men created history: without Moses, the Jews would not have reached the promised land; without Churchill, the British would have given up in 1940.

Modern-day heroes validate this concept, when Iacocca transforms a faltering business, MacArthur emulates military leaders, and Martin Luther King, Jr., leads a civil rights movement (Waite, 2008). At the beginning of the 1930s, during the Great Depression, psychologists studied groups in a consideration of leadership and found that democratic leadership was not only possible but even more effective than a solitary, lone ranger approach to leadership. However, they also discovered that patterns of leadership behavior in small groups were not transferable to large groups or organizations (Rost, 1993).

The 1940s gave way to the trait theories of leadership. Trait leadership theories posited that people were born with certain qualities—intelligence, responsibility, and creativity—that made them leaders. People were asking what traits leaders needed to win the war. The American psychologist Gordon Allport identified almost 18,000 personality traits relevant to leadership. The trait theory focused on analyzing mental, social, and physical characteristics and how those traits interacted within a leader (Matthews, Deary, & Whiteman, 2003).

The 1950s moved into studies of leadership behavior. Some studies were conducted to determine which behaviors contributed to leadership. No key behavioral patterns that made a difference were identified. However, these studies did conclude that leaders were made and not born (Rost, 1993).

The tumultuous 1960s described leadership through Fiedler's contingency theory. This theory argued against a single way of leading, concluding that there is no one best way to organize a corporation, lead a group, or make informed decisions. Contingency theory also purported that an optimal course of action was dependent on internal and external circumstances. Fred Fiedler's studies considered personality and leader characteristics. The Fiedler contingency model also stated that one best leadership model could not exist.

Rather, two factors impact a leader's effectiveness in a situation: leadership style and situational control.

Fiedler believed that leadership style was fixed and could be measured using the scale he developed to do so: the Least Preferred Co-Worker (LPC) Scale. To use the scale (see table 1.1), the respondents identified a least preferred co-worker in a situation and rated how they felt about this co-worker on the LPC. If the score was high, the respondent was generally considered a relationship-oriented leader. If the score was low, the respondent was considered a task-oriented leader.

Relationship-oriented leaders viewed even least preferred co-workers in a positive way, focused on making personal connections, were good at managing and avoiding conflict, and were able to make complex decisions. Task-oriented leaders on the other hand were effective at completing tasks, organizing groups, and getting projects done. However, for task-oriented leaders, building relationships was a low priority.

Fiedler noted that three factors determined the situational control for the leader: the level of trust between the leader and members, the structure of the task—whether the task is clear and structured or vague and unstructured—and the amount of power the leader had to direct the group and provide reward or punishment. A leader who was more trusted, doing a task that was more structured, meant he or she had more power that resulted in a more favorable situation.

One of the criticisms of Fiedler's model was the inflexibility of the model. Because Fiedler believed that leadership was fixed, he also believed that the

Table 1.1. Least Preferred Co-Worker Scale

Unfriendly	1 2 3 4 5 6 7 8	Friendly
Unpleasant	1 2 3 4 5 6 7 8	Pleasant
Rejecting	1 2 3 4 5 6 7 8	Accepting
Tense	1 2 3 4 5 6 7 8	Relaxed
Cold	1 2 3 4 5 6 7 8	Warm
Boring	1 2 3 4 5 6 7 8	Interesting
Backbiting	1 2 3 4 5 6 7 8	Loyal
Uncooperative	1 2 3 4 5 6 7 8	Cooperative
Hostile	1 2 3 4 5 6 7 8	Supportive
Guarded	1 2 3 4 5 6 7 8	Open
Insincere	1 2 3 4 5 6 7 8	Sincere
Unkind	1 2 3 4 5 6 7 8	Kind
Inconsiderate	1 2 3 4 5 6 7 8	Considerate
Untrustworthy	1 2 3 4 5 6 7 8	Trustworthy
Gloomy	1 2 3 4 5 6 7 8	Cheerful
Quarrelsome	1 2 3 4 5 6 7 8	Harmonious

Source: Based on Fiedler (1967).

most effective way to fix a situation was to change the leader. Another criticism of the LPC model was the scale itself. If the person participating fell in the middle range, it was unclear what kind of leadership style was present. And if a person had one really bad experience and completed the scale based on that one least preferred co-worker, the scale may not have given a true picture of the leadership style (MindTools, 2016).

Contingency theories once again concluded that there is no one leadership style. Instead, those being led, the characteristics of the leader, and the situation all contributed to the leader's style and needed to be determined for a more complete understanding of leadership. Fiedler's contingency theory, Hersey and Blanchard's situational theory, and Vroom and Yetton's decision participation contingency theory all support these same ideas. However, aspects of a given situation can be highly subjective and give a false impression of the leader-led situation. The 1970s saw the development of transactional leadership theories.

These theories were viewed as controversial in that they proposed a totalitarian way of responding: obey or else. Transactional leaders were the strongest supporters of this leadership approach, regarding themselves as the reason for being: "I know best" is their mantra and therefore they rule. While this form of leadership was named or identified in the 1970s, this form of leadership has existed throughout the ages. This form of leadership has been described as undignified and used mainly to exploit people. It does not regard, cultivate, or bring out the best in people. Rather, it suppresses human spirit and dignity.

Toward the end of the 1970s, transformational leadership theory emerged. James McGregor Burns in his 1978 book *Leadership* described this theory as a process whereby "leaders and their followers raise one another to higher levels of morality and motivation." Further development of this theory by Bernard Bass (1985) described transformational leaders as models of integrity and fairness, who set goals; had high expectations; encouraged, supported, and recognized others; and moved people to surpass their own personal best. Transformational leadership is still regarded as one of the most important ideas in leadership.

At the turn of the century, the concept of transcendental leadership became another leadership theory. As the word *transcend* suggests, transcendental leadership went beyond former concepts, beliefs, and definitions of leadership. This theory suggested that the leader transcends the ordinary to rise to the level of the peak performer. Qualities of the transcendent leader include the cultivation of generosity, ethics or integrity, patience, humility, unselfishness, and wisdom.

Transcendental leadership theory espoused right effort and persistent practice to cultivate transcendental qualities that led to even greater wisdom.

In various wisdom traditions, the principles may vary slightly, but the movement toward greater wisdom is held constant. Leaders who practiced and cultivated these principles shine from within and cause others to look to them for guidance in many aspects of life.

CHARACTERISTICS OF LEADERS

As each theory developed, a consistent feature was identifying the characteristics of leaders. An Internet search for examples of important leadership characteristics results in a variety of lists:—seven important traits of leadership, top ten qualities that make a leader, twenty-two qualities that make a great leader, ten impressive characteristics that great leaders have (see table 1.2).

The characteristics can be categorized as personal, relational, and organizational. There are characteristics that point to character: honesty, integrity, and authenticity; other characteristics refer to relations with colleagues or co-workers—personableness, open mindedness, flexibility, and positivity. Still other characteristics are those that facilitate working together in the organization—accountability, communication, empowerment, and transparency.

These characteristics point to the theories of leadership that have persisted: the great-man theory with characteristics of confidence and decisiveness; the situational leadership theory that points to focus on ever-changing situations; and the transformational leadership theory that points to empowerment and inspiration.

As the brief history of leadership theories shows, leadership has evolved and continues to evolve. Even so, there is still no one best leader! However, the need for effective leadership also remains. Organizations need to fulfill

Table 1.2. Characteristics of Leaders

• Focus	• Awareness
• Confidence	• Decisiveness
• Integrity	• Empathy
• Inspiration	• Innovation
• Passion	• Confidence
• Decisiveness	• Optimism
• Communication	• Honesty
• Accountability	• Transparency
• Stoicism	• Patience
• Authenticity	• Open mindedness
• Empowerment	• Personableness
• Positivity	• Insightfulness
• Persistence	• Generosity
• Communication	

their fundamental purposes, to seek new ways to remain effective, to deal with crises, to maintain relationships with internal and external customers. Leaders help make these things happen.

THE PHYSICAL CHARACTERISTICS OF LEADERSHIP

Personal leadership characteristics are the responsibility of the leader—to lead self to develop and maintain those essential characteristics; relational characteristics that are necessary to sustain those who sustain the organization; organizational characteristics that help the organization grow and remain true to its fundamental purposes. Having said that, it is important to realize that there are some qualities and characteristics held by a leader over which a leader has no control.

It may seem logical that someone gets a leadership position because of hard work and earning the position as a result, coming up through the ranks, paying one's dues, having prepared for it. However, The Business Insider website points to research about physical attributes that contribute to someone acquiring a hierarchical position. On the site, Drake Baer points out that bosses tend to be male, be tall, be physically fit, and have a tone of voice that influences how he is perceived by others as being able to perform and deserving of the job.

Ruth Moody authored a blog on the mental and physical characteristics of leadership for the Farscape Development site, in which she echoed Baer's conclusions on the importance of psycho-physiological characteristics such as smiling, making eye contact, looking healthy and fit, standing upright, being energetic, laughing, crying, and sounding confident. Even though being mentally prepared and learning new and relevant skills and competencies are important concerns for seeking promotions, there is no doubt that someone who looks the part will be successful.

The Economist even called it the look of a leader (Schumpteter, 2014): "The typical chief executive is more than six feet tall, has a deep voice, a good posture, a touch of grey in his thick, lustrous hair and, for his age, a fit body. Bosses spread themselves out behind their large desks. They stand tall when talking to subordinates. Their conversation is laden with prestige pauses and declarative statements." Even more remarkable, according to the article, is how many bosses still match this ideal. Sounding right also enters into the characteristics. Physical fitness seems undeniable. When potential bosses are overweight, and, regrettably, especially women, they are perceived as being out of control of themselves, and as a result, unable to control or manage others.

The takeaway? *The Economist* article points out that Amy Cuddy of Harvard Business School gave a talk on "power poses" to the 2012 TED Global conference that has since become *TED's second most downloaded talk*. Likewise, a recent book, *Executive Presence*, by Sylvia Anne Hewlett of the Center for Talent Innovation in New York, urges young women to lower the register of their voices, as Margaret Thatcher did, eliminate uptalking and other vocal tics, and look people in the eye when giving presentations.

She advises every would-be manager to work out regularly and look as fit as possible. This may sound like a bit of a cop-out. But the evidence is strong that candidates for top jobs can still be undermined by superficial things like posture and tone of voice. More than a century ago, Oscar Wilde quipped: "It is only shallow people who do not judge by appearances." Unfortunately, those who choose leaders still seem to think this way.

Although they can be described, these are characteristics that cannot be physically imitated in terms of height, weight, and gender. However, this does not discount the importance of paying attention to physical characteristics to the extent possible. There are other characteristics that can serve a leader well, whether in a hierarchical position or with no position at all.

The Entrepreneur website suggests *11 Characteristics of Powerful People You Can Cultivate* (Newlands, 2015). Among the eleven characteristics are confidence and humility, enduring criticism, *looking the part*, *picking a hard seat*, and *carrying heavy objects* (emphasis added). These few recommendations sound like Jeffrey Pfeffer's (2015) *Leadership BS*, which decries the myth that leaders are selected for their qualifications and ability to inspire. Instead, like the nonessential characteristics discussed here, narcissists are chosen because they think more of themselves, are self-aggrandizing, are self-promoting, and are extroverted. As a result, they are more noticeable. They get chosen to fill a position that calls for leadership. Instead, the chosen continues to look like a leader, perhaps with little or no substance.

LEADERSHIP MYTHS DEBUNKED

Pfeffer goes on to describe the sad effects of working under—not for or with—those in hierarchical positions who rely on bullying, often in the form of unilateral decision making, abusive behavior, and stress-inducing situations to maintain and demonstrate the importance of their position. Needed instead are the classical characteristics of modesty, hard work, accountability, devotion to the mission, and loyalty to those who help make the mission a reality.

Leadership—real leadership—develops or is enhanced by attention to the primacy of the vision and mission and how time is used to keep the vision and mission the main thing. Such leadership has a desire and the accompanying will to learn what it means to be mission centered, how to make the mission happen, how to make the organization one that continually improves its fundamental purposes. It means remaining a leader who learns: a learning leader. Constant reflection, sometimes in the form of an inner voice—self-talk—develops a leader who is a problem-solving machine!

These components—vision and mission, time, will to learn, self-talk, and problem solving—will be presented in this work. The goal is to develop a personal commitment to knowing the responsibility and authority they impose, developing the skill to use them productively and ethically, and holding a frame of mind that disposes the leader to caring, to maintaining and strengthening the will to act for the greater good, to behavior and actions congruent with espoused belief.

The components challenge the individual to lead the self. They are like New Year resolutions, easy to make, but usually short lived. Leading self is an imperative to make faithfulness a recurring behavior that happens almost automatically. In an organization, though, it is not enough that only the leader has the knowledge, skills, and dispositions that lead to organizational improvement and continual transformation. History has shown that the *great man*, the *lone ranger*, cannot do it all, cannot do it alone, and cannot offer appearance in place of substance.

Everyone in the organization has a part to play. That means the leader who leads self must also lead others to *lead themselves*. Growing leadership at all levels of the organization is a further imperative to make the vision and mission a reality. The skills for growing leadership in others make leadership visible. The current knowledge culture requires a disposition of respect for those who know more, who have the right to be heard.

Like the members of an orchestra, each with a different instrument that contributes to the beauty of the composition, so, too, are the members of an organization. If any person does not contribute to the good of the organization, why is he or she part of it? On the other hand, if the organization's goals do not serve the goals of the individuals who choose it, why are they part of the organization in the first place? A final imperative is that the leaders who lead self, who lead others to lead themselves, must also work with others for organizational improvement and continual transformation.

It is not enough to have great ideas and make suggestions for continuous improvement of the organization. Such ideas must permeate the entire organization and exist throughout the organization. Turning ideas into reality requires the skills of everyone who will make it happen, whether a worker on the factory floor, a teacher in a classroom, or an organization designer in a business. These skills are fueled by a disposition that no one is working as hard as he or she can to fail!

All want to belong to something larger, something for which they can claim ownership, something they can author—based on the authority that flows from commitment to the vision and mission. The centrality of the vision and mission cannot be underestimated. In effect, the vision and mission are the center of a circle, that single focal point around which all else revolves.

Vision and mission are the impetus for belief and for action. They are not static and do not happen just because they appear in a frame on a wall. They happen because they are supported by actions that are oriented to excellence, the never-ending effort to be better tomorrow than today—not just the excellence that wins awards or accreditations but more often the excellence promoted and sustained by the disposition to constantly surpass one's personal best.

Leading others to lead themselves requires an orientation to dignity, an orientation that prefers capability over dependence, that opposes stereotypical thinking. So often dependence is confused with cooperation and independence for the opposite. The leader who holds the disposition that independence is fundamental to *inter*dependence recognizes that only an independent will can choose to work with others out of commitment rather than compliance that is so often confused with cooperation.

Interdependence is a building block of a mission-centered organization and requires growth-producing interactions rather than peace at any price. Interdependence understands the true meaning and value of conflict—to reveal values at opposite ends of the continuum. Growth-producing interactions require skills that grow from leading self—understanding what is being said from the other person's point of view, acting and not reacting, the ability and desire to find root causes instead of finding someone or something to blame. There needs to be the disposition that sees criticism as information and participation as an ethical imperative.

In summary, leadership means leading self, leading others to lead themselves, leading with others to transform the organization. The qualities and characteristics and components for that to happen will be presented in this book as the knowledge, skills, and dispositions that support the primacy of vision and mission, that support the view that time has a purpose, that learning is an act of will, that self-talk leads to action, that leadership is not a position but the act of problem solving.

REFERENCES

Bass, B. M. (1985). *Leadership and performance beyond expectations*. New York, NY: Free Press.

Burns, J. M. (1978). *Leadership*, 1978. New York: Harper & Row.

Fiedler, F. (1967). *A theory of leadership effectiveness*. New York, NY: McGraw-Hill.

Matthews, G., Deary, I. J., & Whiteman, M. C. (2003). *Personality traits*. New York, NY: Cambridge University Press.

MindTools. (2016). Fiedler's Contingency Model: Matching leadership style to a situation. MindTools. Retrieved from https://www.mindtools.com/pages/article/fiedler.htm

Moody, R. (2010, July 8). The mental and physical characteristics of leadership [blog post]. Retrieved from http://farscapedevelopment.co.uk/the-mental-and-physical-characteristics-of-leadership/

Newlands, M. (2015, September 16). 11 characteristics of powerful people you can cultivate. Entrepreneur. Retrieved from https://www.entrepreneur.com/ARTICLE/249703

Pfeffer, J. (2015). *Leadership BS: Fixing workplace and careeers one truth at a time*. New York, NY: Harper Business.

Rost, J. C. (1993). *Leadership for the twenty-first century*. Westport, CT: Greenwood Publishing Group.

Schumpteter, J. (2014). "The look of a leader." *Economist*. Retrieved from http://www.economist.com/news/business/21620197-getting-top-much-do-how-you-look-what-you-achieve-look-leader

Waite, M. R. (2008). *Fire service leadership: Theories and practices*. Sudbury, MA: Jones and Barlett.

Chapter 2

Secrets of Leadership

Leadership is lifting a person's vision to higher sights, the raising of a person's performance to a higher standard, the building of a personality beyond its normal limitations.

—Peter Drucker

This chapter describes the micro level of leading self as fundamental to the macro level of leading organizations. The goal is to examine how personal mastery leads to professional relationships and ultimately to the collaboration needed for transforming an organization into its grounding purpose.

FORMING AND REFORMING TWENTY-FIRST CENTURY LEADERS

Just how do leaders for the twenty-first century develop? With a constantly changing world bombarded by competing structures, systems, and processes, a new kind of leadership capability to set a course of action and direction needs to be implemented. Leading self, leading others, and leading with others to transform the organization will not happen with a textbook plan in a static classroom.

Leadership for the twenty-first century requires twenty-first century knowledge and skills and the dispositions to support the knowledge and skills. But the big question remains: what do leaders need to know, and what skills do they need for effective leadership? Perhaps a greater question concerns who decides what leaders need to know and what skills they need.

Years of research and literature reviews reveal that finding an all-inclusive list of competencies (knowledge, skills, and dispositions) to develop leaders is not possible. While lists of leadership theories can be studied, leadership surveys can be conducted, and leadership studies can be reviewed, one cannot generate a list of all the knowledge and skills to make a leader.

Furthermore, while some think formal education is a reliable preparation, others believe on-the-job training is critical, while yet others believe personal characteristics contribute to the leader. The reality is that all of these factors contribute to the formation of a leader.

Recognizing that a definitive leadership list does not and cannot exist, a framework of competencies can guide the ever-developing leader in all three aspects of this process: leading self, leading others, and leading with others. The leadership framework structure that encompasses leadership development is a fluid structure with possibilities for relating and integrating each part of the leadership development.

Each of the three levels of leadership development (lead self, lead others, lead with others) will be included in the framework of knowledge, skills, and dispositions. While these components will be developed individually, they cannot be considered as separate entities. Knowledge, skills, and dispositions must be integrated to support leadership development.

Knowledge is a by-product of the process. Textbooks contain answers. Without important questions on which to hang those answers, the information can be sterile and academic.

Skills focus on learning to lead from the position held rather than waiting for a hierarchical position before beginning to lead. Learning has been variously described as a change in behavior or the acquisition of useful programs. If this is so, then learning to lead means there should be some proximate payoff.

Leadership means influence, offering others information with which they can change their minds and behavior. The goal is to describe, apply, and practice leadership knowledge, skills, and dispositions. There are distinctions and relationships between and among power, position, authority, and leadership. While related to and sometimes included in each other, they are not synonymous. Integrated with mission, responsibility, and accountability, these are factors that contribute to an understanding of what it means to be a leader.

Dispositions are inclinations, mental orientations, and states of mind. A leadership disposition is developed by verbalizing the mission, setting goals, creating strategies, developing time-management skills, and making and keeping promises. Developing dispositions requires deliberate practice to develop helpful dispositions such as an orientation toward excellence (wanting always to surpass one's personal best), toward choosing behaviors and participating in those activities that enhance dignity rather than diminish it and those activities that draw people together rather than separate them, discriminate against them, categorize them, or stereotype them. Leading self to develop these dispositions results in practices and skills for leading self, leading others, and leading with others to create the learning organization.

AN ALTERNATIVE LEADERSHIP PERSPECTIVE

Brendan Baker (2012) blogs in The Start of Happiness that personal mastery

> is about our journey towards continuous improvement and seeing life from a different perspective. Personal mastery is guided by principles like purpose, vision, belief, commitment, and knowing oneself. Ultimately, personal mastery is about understanding exactly how you think, why you do things the way you do, having a clear purpose and direction in life and taking steps towards continual learning and development to evolve and enhance oneself.

Baker also notes that personal mastery is not achieved overnight. Personal mastery is ongoing, and one never arrives at the mecca of total personal mastery.

Leading self is like an immigrant's perspective, seeing opportunity in everything and unleashing passionate pursuits while striving for excellence. Few can claim pure American ancestry, and most search for the immigrant ties to a former life, country, and culture. The immigrant comes to a new nation with hopes and dreams for a better tomorrow. The immigrant makes a choice to leave behind the known to seek out the unknown, the unfamiliar. The immigrant sees opportunities that those entrenched in the familiar may miss. Immigrants go down paths that others will not dare to take because they have passion to reach something beyond them. They seize opportunities to build relationships, improve humanity, and promote innovations.

The nature of immigrants is to give—first within their own family and then as a part of the larger family all around them. They give from their harvest and thus cultivate a perpetual harvest. They believe that success comes to those who are surrounded by people who want their success to continue (Llopis, 2015). The immigrant perspective is the secret to leadership for the twenty-first century.

Glenn Llopis (2011) in his article "The Immigrant Perspective on Business Leadership" notes that when his parents came to the United States in the midst of the Castro revolution, the greatest possession they brought with them was their immigrant perspective, which enabled them to adapt and eventually thrive in a new country.

Llopis (2015) lists six values of this immigrant perspective: (1) seeing opportunity in everything; (2) employing a circular vision and anticipating the unexpected; (3) unleashing passionate pursuits while striving for excellence; (4) living with an entrepreneurial spirit with innovation as second nature;

(5) working with a generous purpose; and (6) embracing a cultural promise that leads to leaving a legacy. These values define twenty-first century leadership.

THE MICRO LEVEL OF LEADING SELF

All leadership begins with leading self. If you cannot lead a party of one, you cannot lead others. Personal mastery, leading self, is something everyone wants to achieve.

Recognizing the challenge to personal mastery, all leadership begins with leading self. Looking inward must precede any attempts to look outward.

Table 2.1. Framework for Leading Self

Leading Self

Knowledge	Skills	Dispositions
• Define and differentiate between conflict and "difficult people and situations" • Describe the use of conflict in the learning organization • State the steps of RISC[1] • 12 steps to making change happen • State the 7 habits • State the 5Ss • Vision ~ task • Power ~ position ~ leadership • Mission ~ responsibility ~ goals ~ objectives • Intrapersonal and interpersonal skills • Builders of and barriers to capability • Influence of self-talk on behavior • 90–10 principles • 80–20 principles • 70–30 principles • Change others' behavior by changing our own • Choices and postures • Roles in groups	• Use of RISC • Create a graphic representing the mission • 5Ss • Leadership style and leading with style image builders; image killers empowering, de-powering constructive use of criticism • Enlarge options between stimulus and responses • Choose a posture • Choose a perception • Manage time • Lead self • Metacognition • Time management • Group member • Time management: make the important and urgent, schedule priorities; don't prioritize schedules • Communicate leadership • Use graphics • Application • Synthesis • Evaluation • Practice the 7 habits	• Responsible self-direction • See the half-full glass • 7 habits: • Begin with the end in mind • Sharpen the saw • A proactive frame of mind • Don't let the urgent drive out the important; make the important urgent • Build a cathedral • Hold opposing viewpoints (old lady-young lady) • Thoughts are things: positive or negative vision • An ethical platform supported by dignity, excellence, connectedness • Victimhood is optional • Change is inevitable; growth is a choice • Power is not a four-letter work • Work expands to fill the time available

[1] Report, Impact, Suggest, Consequence.

Peter Senge (1990) popularized the idea of personal mastery in his book *The Fifth Discipline*. He describes this as the discipline of personal growth and learning. Personal mastery begins with a personal vision—an image of a desired future—seeking what matters most and determining the purpose for that vision. Personal mastery is leading self through intensive self-awareness.

Awareness of self leads to mindfulness—the ability to recognize how one's thoughts and actions contribute to everyday decisions. Choices are made based on recognizing and regulating self. Being aware of self further contributes to the next level of leadership—leading others—as the self becomes aware of the impact those choices have on others (see table 2.1).

THE MID LEVEL OF LEADING OTHERS

Leading others is a mismeme. No one can make anyone do anything. The only possible way to lead others is to get others to want to follow. Consider the people you would follow anywhere. Then consider why you would follow those people. What characteristics and ideals come to mind that best describe those who inspire others to follow?

One description that comes to mind is *Sherpa*. *The American Heritage Dictionary* (2011) provides this definition: "A member of a traditionally Buddhist people of Tibetan ancestry living on the southern side of the Himalaya Mountains in Nepal and the Indian state of Sikkim. In modern times Sherpas have achieved renown as high-altitude porters and expert guides on Himalayan mountaineering expeditions." Sherpas inspire confidence, and these expert guides are the ones to follow when confronted with insurmountable challenges.

Leaders and those aspiring to lead must keep in mind the importance of leadership. Oftentimes, a leader becomes so caught up in the new job and dealing with the challenges in the new position that the leader forgets to connect with those who are a part of the organization. The leader must build the business but also needs to lead its people. Leaders recognize the importance of attracting the right followers. This requires a shared commitment to the vision of the leader. People want to have a sense of where they are going and why this destination is attractive. Pursuing a new journey requires trust in the one who is leading the way.

Communication is critical between followers and leaders. Communication not only tells what is happening or what is expected but also reveals the energy and enthusiasm that is present or absent in the pursuit of the vision. Communication must be consistent and effective. Leaders who communicate in words and deeds attract others.

Like the immigrant perspective, leadership has circular vision. Leaders have a sixth sense in anticipating false promises and unexpected outcomes.

Table 2.2. Framework for Leading Others

Leading Others

Knowledge	Skills	Dispositions
• Teams ~ groups • Conflict ~ difficult people and situations • Motivation and self-interest • Motivation mismemes • Talent • Group dynamics take place one person at a time • Self-interest • Positioning • Knowledge is the by-product of the process • Relationships are all there is • How thoughts are things; how self-talk and language influence behavior • 80–20 principle • 70–30 principle • components of a brain compatible environment • learning is the acquisition of useful programs, a change in behavior • the ellipse • the axes	• Communication: speaking, writing, teaching, convening, listening, reading • How to communicate • Leadership, mission, policy and standards • 30–3–30; how to get your "stuff" on the fridge • design and conduct productive meetings • provide information with which others can change their minds and behavior • team building • control ~ autonomy ~ cooperation • conformity ~ internalization • maintenance-producing interactions ~ growth-producing interactions • uncover and discover talent . . . from talent • delegate by design, not by dumping • positioning • verbal self-defense • do it with data • gathering perceptions • seek common ground • design and conduct a change process for the school using the 12 steps • get and give feedback • using criticism • moving from conformity to norms to internalization of norm; from maintenance-producing interactions to growth-producing interactions	• Dissatisfaction with what is the beginning of improvement • No one is working as hard as he or she can to fail • Can't make anyone do anything ~ no one can make me do anything either • Teaching role of leadership • Future orientation • There is no truth, only truth as it is perceived • Criticism is information • If we treat others as they are, they will remain so; if we treat them as they might be, they will become so • External supervision may correct errors, but only internal supervision can prevent them • Don't freeze people where they are • Life is a movie, a test is a snapshot

Where others see borders, this perspective allows leaders to see opportunities. They become proficient at anticipating and managing issues before they arise (Llopis, 2011). This sixth sense engenders feelings of confidence in those with whom they associate.

Leading others flows from the immigrant's perspective of a generous purpose. Just as the immigrant is raised to consider the needs of others, so leaders recognize that they are part of a larger family as they work with others to give from their own harvest and thus produce an ever-growing harvest with others. Leaders lead by an example of their own hard work, their commitment to the vision, and the level of respect they give to those with whom they associate.

Keeping in mind that no one can force followership helps the leader recognize that the real leader is the guide on the side, the Sherpa, the servant leader, the teacher. Leading others is all about helping others to lead themselves (see table 2.2).

THE MACRO LEVEL OF LEADING WITH OTHERS TO TRANSFORM THE ORGANIZATION

Leading self and leading others provide the foundation for the macro level in transforming an organization. Often, the CEO of the organization is regarded as the leader for the whole organization. However, several issues result when one person is regarded as the leader. All organizations must be in the process of change. No organization can stand still and expect to grow, thrive, and make a difference. Complacency in an organization leads to stagnation, which results in decay.

The process of change is messy. The Center for Creative Leadership found that a simple recipe for change does not work and a quick fix for transformation is not a reality. Five reasons are given suggesting why change of leadership is not sufficient: "1) Bigger minds are needed to keep pace with rapidly changing reality. 2) Change requires new mindsets not just new skills. 3) Hidden assumptions and beliefs must be unearthed. 4) Organization change requires leaders to change. 5) It takes a new kind of hard work. Stop calling them 'soft' skills" (McGuire, Paulus, Pasmore, & Rhodes, 2015, p. 4).

No one person can be the only change agent in an organization. In organizations that believe the CEO, the president, or the superintendent can bring about change, disaster happens. A collaborative leadership culture must be in place for transforming an organization into its grounding purpose.

The Center for Creative Leadership describes three levels of the hierarchy of leadership culture: dependent, independent, and interdependent, with each level more successfully responding to deeper challenges. Dependent leadership culture holds only people in authority responsible for transformation.

Independent leadership culture assumes that leadership emerges as needed from several individuals based on knowledge and expertise. Interdependent leadership culture views leadership "as a collective activity that requires mutual inquiry, learning, and a capacity to work with complex challenges" (McGuire et al., 2015, p. 6).

Sometimes, a hierarchical leader sees dependence as cooperation. Perhaps a weak person in a leadership position needs to feel needed. Then, when a subordinate waits for direction and instruction, that may appear to be cooperation when in fact it is a sop to the needs of the person in charge.

For that same kind of leader, independence is seen as obstinate and uncooperative. It takes a leader, a real leader to recognize that independence is essential. It is the process of arriving at independence that can be messy. One need only think of adolescents trying to establish selfhood to appreciate the pains of growing into independence.

However, it is the independent person who is best able to choose to work interdependently with others. Interdependence results from mutual reliance on members that differs from reliance in a dependent relationship. Independence is required for proactivity, responsible self-direction, commitment, and contribution. Interdependence results in the productivity of synergy.

Leaders will need to be mindful of the elliptical nature of the organization. The success of each individual must be integrated into the success of the company. The leaders of the future will lead leaders not followers. Leading others to lead themselves is to lead leaders. The action that develops leaders is a hallmark of generative leadership. The commitment to the vision fuels the generativity of leading others to lead themselves. Connecting to other leaders in service to accomplishing the vision develops the strength and courage to live the mission.

Leadership of the future is the legacy of today's leadership. Those at all levels of leadership who want a part to play in creating the future need to take some steps to do so, to leave the legacy that will bear their imprint. Today's leaders will create the future by supporting those with the commitment and accountability for the vision. Positive self-talk needs to become standard operating procedure, and leaders will need to be mindful of the elliptical nature of the organization.

To move from leading self (personal mastery) to transforming the organization requires leadership—not just *a* leader! The heroic figure at the top of the bureaucratic pyramid cannot make this happen in isolation. The shift must be to an intentional collaborative activity. And yet while the value of the once-highly-regarded superman or superwoman is questioned, the need for the leader has never been more imperative (see table 2.3).

This chapter introduced the three levels of leadership—leading self, leading others, and leading with others. This overview gave a glimpse into each

Table 2.3. Framework for Leading the Organization

Leading with Others to Transform the Organization

Knowledge	Skills	Dispositions
• Chaos theory • Systems theory • Systemic skills: cause ~ effect: not necessarily related in location and time • Privileges ~ responsibility • Authority ~ responsibility • Authority without position • Customer focus • Oriented to learning, excellence, connectedness • Adaptable, flexible • Structure influences behavior • Internalization + growth-producing interactions = organizational transformation (transformation of structures) • Knowledge is a by-product of the process	• Engage stakeholders • Seek common ground • Designing organizational tasks • Small incremental change early enough in a large process produces substantial results • Begin with the end in mind • Get the right people in the room • Synergize	• All change begins with a change of mind • Relationships are all there is, the flap of the butterfly wing; vision is an invisible field • Dignity: doing good leads to work excellence: surpass yesterday's best for organizational learning • Connectedness: to each other, to the past and present, for the future • Information is to an organization what blood is to the body • Participation is an ethical imperative

level and how the micro level of leading self lays the groundwork for moving to the next two levels. Within this chapter, the leadership framework showed how the three components of knowledge, skills, and dispositions are outlined for developing levels of leadership.

REFERENCES

American Heritage Dictionary of the English Language, 5th ed. (2011). New York, NY: Houghton Mifflin Harcourt.

Baker, B. (2012, August 9). What is personal mastery—A look into personal development from a new perspective [blog]. The start of happiness. Retrieved from http://www.startofhappiness.com/what-is-personal-mastery/

Llopis, G. (2011, October). The immigrant perspective on business leadership. Glenn Llopis Group. Retrieved from http://www.glennllopisgroup.com/pdf/Immigrant%20Perspective%20Whitepaper.pdf

Llopis, G. (2015, April 1). 6 characteristics that define 21st century leadership. Forbes. Retrieved from http://www.perspectiveonathletics.com/6-characteristics-that-define-21st-century-leadership/

McGuire, J. B., Paulus, C. P., Pasmore, W., & Rhodes, G. B. (2015). Transforming your organization. Center for Creative Leadership. Retrieved from http://insights.ccl.org/wp-content/uploads/2015/04/TYO.pdf

Senge, P. M. (1990, revised 2006). *The fifth discipline: The art and practice of the learning organization.* New York: Doubleday.

Chapter 3

Growing into Leadership

The task of the leader is to get his people from where they are to where they have not been.

—Henry Kissinger

Many people think of leadership as getting others to do what the leader wants them to do. What leadership actually does is help others lead themselves and together lead an organization to fulfill its fundamental purpose. People need to know this because leadership has evolved over time to a state of participantship. Everyone wants to be involved in the decisions and changes that affect them.

Simply, even simplistically, leaders get things done! If that is the case, then leadership abounds! Parents and teachers, preachers and believers, fund-raisers, telemarketers, CEOs, chairpersons are among those who have to get things done—and do so! So are librarians, auto mechanics, baggers in a grocery store, and those who deliver the mail because they get things done, too. So are Sherpas, taxi and bus drivers, mail room sorters, and data input clerks. So many others can be added to the list.

The leaders listed here are actually grouped—the first set are leaders by position; they get things done because their jobs require it. The second set comprises those who help others get things done. The third set comprises people who do the work that helps those who help others get things done. If leaders get things done, then all are leaders, and, they have choices about how to get the work done.

All leaders have to determine how they will make decisions, manage their time, and communicate and team with others. Other decisions they have to make are related to knowing enough about their jobs to do them with confidence and a positive attitude, to considering their work a service to others, and to determining how well and how effectively they will get things done.

There is still one more thing to think about the matter of leadership—are there any followers? Parents and teachers automatically have followers, as do CEOs of companies. How about mail room clerks and data entry workers? Who follows them? Furthermore, do those in these positions consider themselves leaders in the traditional sense of the word—those in a position of authority over others? Do they even think of their influence—a hallmark of leadership, their ability to influence others? Do they want to be leaders and to develop their leadership?

Those who want to be leaders, who think of themselves as having influence over others, who want to make a difference, are the audience for this book—especially parts II, III, and IV. Those who are leaders by position or by influence, those who want to take on the challenges, responsibility, and authority of leadership will benefit by reading about leading self, leading others—yes, but leading others to lead themselves—and leading *with* others to make the difference, to lead an organization. There will be ideas for developing and enhancing leadership.

Leadership development requires willingness, not just readiness (Lake, 2015). It means walking alongside someone for an extended period of time to help that person learn the skills of leading. Leadership development sees potential in others and helps them develop it to the greatest extent possible. Developing as a leader means taking on the tasks of leadership, leading from the position one has, instead of waiting to have the title or position of a leader. Becoming a leader means developing or enhancing one's confidence and competence and making the investment in time, learning, and relationships that will get things done.

One Internet search for the term *leadership* resulted in 783 million entries (in 0.59 seconds, by the way!). The first page of results presents links to defining leadership, information about leadership, the psychology of leadership, the most important leadership competencies, the top ten—and the top twenty-two—qualities that make a great leader! Page 5 in the 783 million search returns talks about leadership in the digital age, strategic leadership, leadership community, implementation and impact of leadership, and even wonderful leadership. Further searches recommend management, importance, and types of leadership. Page 10 suggests that the searcher find out the leadership traits needed *right now*, the ten mistakes leaders have to avoid, more definitions, and five lessons for success this time.

Naturally, there are naysayers about leadership. A search for lies about leadership resulted in 13,600,000 webpages in a little less time, 0.39 seconds. This time, the links point out seven leadership lies, the ten most believed lies, and eight great lies; page 5 mentions four planning lies and five leadership lies, and page 10 talks about who lies!

So what can be known about leadership? Mostly what it is for, its qualities and characteristics, its importance, common lies, and misconceptions. This book takes the approach that there is leadership everywhere. For those who want to be a leader, the basic premise is that it is possible to grow in and into leadership and develop or enhance characteristics and qualities to become a leader by position or a better leader in the position one holds or for a position aspired for. Again, in a simple, and perhaps in a simplistic form, leaders get things done. That is why Hitler and Mother Teresa are both leaders. The secret is what gets done!

The journey then to leadership growth and development begins with the longest journey, the one Hammarskjöld (1982) calls *the journey inward*. Having personal goals for health and exercise—often New Year resolutions—and professional or personal goals of promotions or a new job or a larger apartment all require leading a party of one: self! The question is, if you can't lead a party of one, how can you hope to lead others?

THE CHALLENGE TO BE MORE THAN ORDINARY

Many people think of leadership as getting others to do what the leader wants them to do, basing this belief on classical ideas about leadership. Historically, leaders have used legitimate power—being able to tell people what to do and expecting compliance because of the superior and inferior positions of the parties involved. Likewise, coercive power required submission and compliance because of the ability to punish and reward. Leadership is conceived differently today. In fact, when current events reveal a coercive type of leadership, there is a fundamental concern about whether a forceful use of power should be tolerated.

If leadership gets things done, then one of the things that *should* get done is helping others lead themselves and together lead an organization to fulfill its fundamental purpose. People need to know this because leadership has evolved over time to a state of participantship. Everyone wants to be involved in the decisions and changes that affect them.

The next part of this chapter examines the role of vision and mission as well as the relation of responsibility and authority that arise from vision and mission. The chapter will consider how leadership and power relate and how leading from one's current position is preferred to waiting to hold a position from which to lead. As Kissinger noted, "The task of the leader is to get his people from where they are to where they have not been." Vision, mission, and power together give strength to others so they may stand on their own.

Chapter 3

THE POWER OF VISION

The well-known biblical admonition of Proverbs 29:18, that "without vision, the people perish," points to the need for some source of guidance; for some Christians, the proverb points to the need for leaders to be guided by a focus, a destination, a goal for the journey. Some of the sources of leadership point to the need for vision. Bass (1990) believed that transformational leadership required sharing the vision and occurred when "leaders broaden and elevate the interests of their employees, when they generate awareness and acceptance of the purposes and mission of the group, and when they stir their employees to look beyond their own self-interest for the good of the group" (p. 19).

THE EFFECTS OF A VISION

In a simple form (again), vision is a mental picture of something that has not yet occurred but hoped for. Its power lies in what is hoped for. The Internet is replete with stories of successful grand failures that illustrate the power of vision: Walt Disney was fired from a newspaper because he "lacked imagination and had no good ideas." Oprah Winfrey, at the age of twenty-two, was fired from her job as a television reporter because she was "unfit for TV" (Gillett, 2015). Steven Spielberg was rejected from film school, not once, not twice, but three times. Michael Jordan was cut from his high school basketball team. Thomas Edison failed some 10,000 times before successfully inventing the light bulb. How is it, then, that they are known for the very things at which they *failed*?

Jim Carrey wrote himself a $10 million check that he postdated by ten years. He was able to cash that check. Mary Higgins Clark had her books rejected forty times in the 1950s. In the 1990s, she cashed a check for $64 million. James Joyce's epic masterpiece *Ulysses*, regarded as one of the greatest Irish novels, was repeatedly rejected by baffled publishers before finally being published in a tiny edition in Paris in 1922 by his friend Sylvia Beach's Shakespeare & Co bookshop: a copy of the first edition sold a few years ago for £275,000. J.K. Rowling posted her initial rejections; in 2010, long after she came off the dole, she was listed among the world's wealthiest women.

VISION-INSPIRED RESULTS

The persistence and consistence of these successful failures point to the power of the vision these people held for what they saw in the future. They then created the conditions that produced in the future what they personally lacked in the present. These are personal and individual stories. Known variously as *grit, mindset, getting things done, smarter, faster, better*, a vision of *what can be* seems to be the power behind behavior leading to a desired result. If it is that power, then getting to the vision provides a kind of authority to get to it, a kind of responsibility to produce what is needed to meet the goal.

There are just as many stories of business and school turnarounds that are inspirational. As Lauren in *Kinky Boots* noted, "maybe you judge what you leave behind by what you inspire in other people." Apple, once on the brink of bankruptcy, is now among the most valuable companies in the world. FedEx staved off bankruptcy with winnings from a bet. The ubiquitous Starbucks facing a downturn in 2008 renewed itself. Bacon—yes those salty strips of pork belly—reinvented itself, no longer just a fat, but as a flavor enhancer for everything from chocolate to ice cream.

Some of the same stories have their sources in school turnarounds based on the vision of what could be. Robert Kennedy, paraphrasing Shaw, gives a rationale: "Some men see things as they are and say, why; I dream things that never were and say, why not." A collection from *Education Week*'s "Turnaround Schools" (2017) retell some of the success stories.

Philadelphia experimented with outside management of schools for over a decade. Through the Renaissance Schools Initiative, low-performing schools were identified and assisted internally and externally for turnaround overhaul. Superintendent Arlene Ackerman aggressively reshaped into charters, with operators required to "restart" more than a dozen struggling schools. Pouring resources into eighteen district-managed "Promise Academies" along with Mastery Charter Schools created opportunities to expand.

In Colorado, the state's 2008 Innovation Schools Act gave chosen schools greater flexibility by waiving certain state statutes, district policies, and union contract provisions to help boost student achievement even in the face of pushback. Principal Keith Look and his team at the former Shawnee High School in Louisville, Kentucky, worked to transform the long-troubled campus by replacing more than half the teachers, using data more to pinpoint students' weaknesses and to adjust instruction, and reinventing itself as the Academy@Shawnee.

Chicago, considered a national model for its turnaround program, has also had some success raising test scores in spite of various hurdles yet to be overcome. A sweeping and ambitious turnaround plan for schools in the newer neighborhoods around Denver International Airport led to a failed recall effort against the school board president in the spring of 2016. It also became a major issue in the mayoral election, even though the Denver mayor holds no legal authority over the school district. The plan passed Denver's divided school board on a 4–3 vote in April, but the battle was far from over. Denver held pivotal elections for three school board seats in November, and the Far Northeast Denver turnaround plan was sure to be a major issue, but the Denver school package has since passed.

Stories abound. For this book, the stories are used as a touchstone to illustrate the importance of vision to drive continuous improvement. The vision works for New Year resolutions and business turnarounds, for personal improvement, and for organizational improvement. In fact, this book proposes that organizational transformation is the result of personal mastery, that those who lead organizations to success also believe that their own transformations are essential to helping others commit to the vision and in the process leading the organization to its success.

WHAT'S MISSION GOT TO DO WITH IT

Another simplistic statement: mission is how the vision gets accomplished. And like vision, it becomes a "constitution to live by" (Covey, 1991). Vision is the great *why*—why should anyone care? Why will the vision make a difference? Mission is the *how*. What must be done daily to make the vision a reality? A vision is a pipe dream. A mission is the nuts and bolts of the transformational machinery. As with leadership turnaround stories, there are sources for ideas about vision and mission. For this book, vision and mission form the underpinnings of leadership. They are the basis of how to use time, provoke the will to learn, are the inner voice of self-talk, and at the same time are the source and solution of problems.

Leading self is the foundation of leading others, not to do what the leader says to do but rather to lead themselves so they too possess the fundamentals and can lead from the positions they have to promote the organization's well-being, its learning, and its purpose. In fact, engaging others, the internal and external stakeholders, to create and sustain the mission and vision means respecting the part they play in the ownership of the mission and vision. More minds may more accurately reflect perceptions of the organization and its value beyond maintaining its own existence.

When internal stakeholders of the organization have a clear idea of the mission and how it contributes to the vision and are conscious of the values promoted by the organization, then communication is facilitated, management practice and action are enacted, and short- and long-term goals and actions are kept in sync by their compatibility with the long-range vision and the mission to meet the vision. Keeping the mission alive in service of the vision is what keeps the mission statement from being just a framed document on an office wall.

Glenn Smith's (2016) executive coaching website (http://www.glennsmithcoaching.com/) summarizes the value of a mission into seven reasons to have one: (1) to determine organizational direction, (2) to focus on the future, (3) to provide a template for decision making, (4) to achieve alignment, (5) to recognize and use helpful change, (6) to shape strategy, and (7) to facilitate evaluation and improvement.

A clear vision and mission provide a starting point for what to do when you don't know what to do. The challenge of finding out is a desirable one; it leads to the will to act because it holds promise. The mission statement serves as the North Star, the star that keeps everyone looking in the same direction.

The mission focuses the organization on the preferred future, also known as the vision. The mission describes what we are doing today that will lead to the preferred future tomorrow, next year, the next decade, and hopefully into the next century.

The mission provides the framework for all decision making, allowing leaders to set boundaries and delegate responsibility as well as authority. It keeps the organization moving forward on the right path together—with all members of the team and organization. The mission can even provide a bridge to needed change as the members look to the mission to identify the value for the change.

The mission shapes the strategies the organization needs to set out to accomplish what the organization represents. The mission facilitates what needs to be measured and improved. A clear mission describes what the organization will accomplish and watches it happen.

A mission and vision will be successful only if all members of the organization commit to the success and internalize them. This full commitment is where the power of the mission and vision begin. This power gets people from where they are to where they have never been.

Parts II, III, and IV explore the knowledge, skills, and dispositions needed to lead self, to lead others to lead themselves, and together to lead in transforming the organization. Mission and vision, using time, the will to learn, self-mastery through self-talk, and problem solving move leaders from dependence, to independence, to interdependence.

REFERENCES

Bass, B. M. (1990). From transactional to transformational leadership: Learning to share the vision. *Organizational Dynamics* 18(3), 19–31.

Covey, S. R. (1991). *The 7 habits of highly effective people.* New York, NY: Simon & Schuster.

Education Week. (2017, January 29). Turnaround schools. *Education Week.* Retrieved from http://www.edweek.org/ew/collections/turnaround-schools/

Gillett, R. (2015). How Walt Disney, Oprah Winfrey, and 19 other successful people rebounded after getting fired. Inc.com. Oct. 7, 2015.

Hammarskjöld, D. (1982). *Markings,* Vol. 30699. New York, NY: Ballantine Books.

Lake, M. (2015, January 1). Is what you're doing really leadership development. *Leadership Development*. Retrieved from http://www.maclakeonline.com/category/leadership-development/page/8/

Smith, G. (2016, March 29). Seven reasons your company needs a clear, written mission statement. *Marketing and Business Tips*. Retrieved from http://www.glennsmithcoaching.com/7-reasons-your-company-needs-clear-written-mission-statement/

Part II

LEADING SELF

All leadership begins with leading oneself. Before anyone can lead someone else, the first step to leadership is knowing how to lead yourself and what makes you a leader.

This part addresses how one grows into self-leadership. The core of all leadership is the mission and vision of the leader. Recognizing what is your passion and what you are willing to do to achieve that passion shapes the leader and gives the leader a direction. With a clear personal vision and mission, leaders make decisions about how they will use time, what they will do to continue learning, how they will develop personal mastery through self-talk, and what they will do to face and solve daily challenges and problems. This part includes knowledge, skills, and dispositions for leading self.

Chapter 4

The Secret of Getting Ahead Is Getting Started

I cannot trust a man to control others who cannot control himself.

—Robert E. Lee

"In case of emergency, air masks will drop from the ceiling. If you are traveling with a child, please put on your own mask before helping the child." These all-too-familiar instructions heard on all flights can be particularly jarring to the parent, teacher, or caregiver who naturally would want to help the child before helping himself or herself. These instructions make perfect sense, though, because an adult cannot be helpful to a child if the adult is incapacitated.

Leading self can be regarded in the same selfish way. How is leading self a necessity to effectively leading others and leading the organization? Leaders of schools, school districts, companies, and organizations have had to respond to global, social, economic, and educational trends by using the wisdom of tradition to meet current challenges. This chapter will consider what it means to lead self and the knowledge required for leading self.

Such knowledge will require leaders to lead from the positions they currently hold as they prepare for the positions they wish to hold. Such knowledge includes the relation of vision and mission, the use of time, learning how to learn, using self-talk, and holding a problem-solving frame of mind. This chapter will introduce knowledge about the mathematics of leadership and the influence of self-talk on behavior.

DREAMING THE DREAM

Henrietta, like Mother Teresa, had a vision. For more than fifteen years, Henrietta worked as an assistant dietician in a hospital in rural Pennsylvania.

In addition to her day job, Henrietta also was actively involved in her church group. Among the many activities within the church, she would visit the homebound. During one of those visits, Agnes, one of the homebound Henrietta visited regularly, asked her to stop by her next-door neighbor Charlie to cheer him up. Henrietta's visit to Charlie changed her life.

Upon entering Charlie's very neat and tidy apartment, Henrietta was greeted warmly and offered a cup of coffee. As they sat in the kitchen with their cup of instant coffee, Charlie opened the refrigerator to get the milk. To Henrietta's surprise, the tiny refrigerator was practically empty. Without wanting to ask too many invading questions, she made a mental note of the situation.

The following day, as she was cleaning up in the hospital kitchen, Henrietta shared Charlie's situation with her supervisor, Vincetta. As they were inventorying the leftover food from the day, the food that never left the kitchen, Henrietta posed the question: "Can I make a plate to take to Charlie and one for myself to join with him?"

Hospital servings are commonly "one size fits all." This implies throwing away a certain amount of food. Food that has been out on a department floor or returned by a patient cannot be reused for other patients, while food that has not yet left the kitchen does not have the same restrictions. As Vincetta considered the request, she told Henrietta to make the two plates. This simple act was the embryo of Henrietta's vision—to make food available to those who need it and the start of the local meals on wheels and eventually the first soup kitchen in the area.

Henrietta worked with Vincetta to procure needed permissions from the hospital and the local authorities to use the leftover food to feed the less fortunate. Within the first three months, Henrietta was providing daily meals for forty-four people in the local community. Within the year, she recognized that the need to feed people in the area was far larger than this undertaking could handle. The number who needed a hot meal each day had grown to seventy-five. One good deed led to another, and Henrietta soon had ten members of her church assisting with delivering these meals five days a week.

When Henrietta took steps to establish meals on wheels for the homebound, authorities blocked her endeavors with unsubstantiated information stating there were no homeless hungry individuals in the area. Within those first three months, forty-four people were requesting a hot meal on a daily basis. Within the year, the demand for a hot meal had grown to such proportions that Henrietta recognized the need to establish a center that could better serve the needs of the people. Not only did they need a hot meal each day but they also needed clothing, household supplies, and in some instances, temporary shelter.

As the numbers grew, the hospital could not provide all the meals that were needed. Henrietta started making contacts in the community for food donations, which became plentiful. Storage for the food, a place to cook the food, and a place to serve the food became the next challenge. Within that first year, Henrietta gathered the resources needed to establish what is known today as St. Anthony's Center. In addition to the soup kitchen that served as many as 225 people a day, the Center grew to provide

- a free medical clinic facility;
- clothing, pre-owned furniture, and appliances for those in need;
- shelter during disasters; and
- retreats for overnight and single-day sessions.

All this became a reality because of Henrietta's vision nearly thirty-seven years ago. Today, the Center continues to provide for the needs of the less fortunate, with several regular staff members and more than 100 volunteers under the oversight of a volunteer board of directors.

MISSION BORN OF VISION

Long before she established St. Anthony's Center, Henrietta had a vision to relieve the hunger of those in her hometown. She worked as a dietician in a hospital and from the position she had, she was already easing the physical hunger for patients. In addition, she visited the homebound and provided them with companionship, comfort, and a network of providers.

A vision looks into the future and visualizes anticipated results of the mission (Jones, 1996). Covey (1989) described it as beginning with the end in mind. A successful component of leadership is the ability to visualize and articulate a possible future. A vision without a task is a daydream. As seen from the research studies of Mayo and Nohria (2005), vision that is separated from context can produce erratic and unpredictable results. The researchers found that CEOs who failed either lacked vision or lacked the ability to bring the vision to reality.

Leadership success always starts with vision. Captivating visions can change the world. Persisting in bringing them to reality can be a challenge, one that is extremely difficult (Ryan, 2009). Leading self is a personal experience that begins with a vision of a preferred future and a mission and drive to make that future a reality.

Jones (1996) suggested that a vision is a sustaining force and a power that propels. In developing a vision of the preferred future, visions are written in the present tense as if already accomplished. Vision statements include a variety of activities and time frames and enough descriptive detail to connect the vision to reality.

Stephen Covey (1989) in *The 7 Habits of Highly Effective People* notes that a personal mission statement is the most effective way to begin with the end in mind. He says the mission statement "focuses on what you want to be (character) and to do (contributions and achievements) and on the values or principles upon which being and doing are based" (p. 106). Creating mission and vision statements are exercises in recognizing your own goals and life purposes.

WHAT LEADERS DO AND HOW AND WHEN THEY DO IT

Just as self-discipline is the key to success, the lack of self-discipline is sure to lead to failure. Brian Tracy (2010) in his book *No Excuses! The Power of Self-Discipline* suggests that the strongest enemies of success are the path of least resistance and the expediency factor.

The path of least resistance leads down the road of the easy way out in most situations. Following it is generally paved with excuses for why the situation is not your fault and therefore for your right to choose what is easier than what is necessary to achieve real success.

The expediency factor goes one step beyond the path of least resistance. One who follows this pathway chooses to act according to self-interest with minimal regard for what is right. In addition to getting things in the fastest and easiest way possible, consideration is not given to long-term consequences of this kind of behavior.

Use of time is a choice. Peter Drucker (2008) says that you cannot manage time; you can only manage yourself. Time cannot be saved. The Pareto principle states that 20 percent of what you do is worth 80 percent of what you value—the mathematics of leadership. If you value reading, consider the amount of time you actually read. Where you spend your time and your money gives you a clear insight into the values you have established in your life. Leading self requires a regular examination of your calendar. Learning to set priorities requires developing a habit of asking "Is this the best use of my time?"

In this digital age of instantaneous connection and response, developing a habit of time choice is critical. Do you answer a text message every time one is sent to your phone? Statistically, texting is faster and more economical than phone calls; however, with the average number of text messages received daily at more than fifty, the amount of time wasted through distraction from the task at hand generates hours of non-productivity.

Leading self toward growth requires the discipline of managing time. David, in his carefree days as a self-contained fourth grade teacher, scoffed at the suggestion of using a calendar to track how he was spending his time. Once he became a building principal, the calendar became his biggest time manager.

> People compete for your time when you are a principal. That is not a negative reality—it is merely a reality. As an educational leader, I have to be more accessible and less self-preserving. Every day at school begins with my calendar—what are my most important activities, who are the people with whom I will meet today, what are my negotiable and non-negotiable times today.
>
> I have created an assessment calendar for my teachers. Every state and local assessment date is included in the calendar for the entire year. I helped teachers manage their curriculum for the year using this assessment calendar.
>
> Going from no calendar to a calendar that allows me to foster great collaboration is quite a journey. As a learning leader, my time management has permitted me to not only lead myself, but also lead the whole school. (Personal communication, August 2016)

The discipline required for time management results in a more focused self. Prioritizing tasks can lead to giving 100 percent of attention to whatever task is to be undertaken. Remaining focused without succumbing to replying to emails and text messages, getting a snack, or turning on the television results in better planning, concentration, and confidence in one's ability to succeed.

Julie Jackson, principal of North Star Elementary School in Newark, New Jersey, is considered by some a miracle worker. At the start of the school year, one of eighty kindergarten students could read and most of the others knew only a few letters of the alphabet. After one year in her school, where most students qualify for free or reduced lunch, Julie's students no longer lagged behind, but rather surpassed their peers. On the Terra Nova tests, her students scored in the 99th percentile in reading, language arts, and math.

This is not an isolated situation. Julie has led the opening of two more schools with the same results. Julie Jackson knows how to spend her time and how to lead others to do the same to ensure learning for all students. Exceptional school leaders succeed because they know how to use their time and make choices about what they do and when they will do it (Bambrick-Santoyo, 2012).

LEARNING TO LEARN

"Knowledge and skill are the keys to the twenty-first century. Becoming the best person you can possibly be and moving to the top of your field require the application of self-discipline throughout your life. Mental fitness is like physical fitness: If you want to achieve either, you must work at it all your life" (Tracy, 2010, p. 83). Learning is an ongoing process. The knowledge and skills of today will keep you afloat for today. To move into tomorrow requires acquisition of new knowledge and skill every day.

Leading self requires a critical eye to move from good to great. Recognizing that learning is an ongoing commitment is a first step in the learning process. Determining what you need to learn and how you can learn what you need to learn is the greater challenge. The secret is the desire to learn.

In the field of education, degrees and certifications commonly are expected. Few teachers in classrooms or leaders in schools arrived there without the proper credentials. Practicing teachers and administrators participate in mandated professional development. State regulations require educators to update their knowledge and skills in their field as well as in their practice. However, too often, professional development becomes drive-by staff development that is not selected by the educator and all too often never finds application back at the school.

All educators—and especially those in leadership—need goals to identify next steps toward personal and professional growth. Charles Duhigg (2016) in his book *Smarter, Faster, Better: The Secrets of Being Productive in Life and Business* describes two types of goals: stretch goals and SMART goals. He describes stretch goals as goals that are so big, ambitious, and audacious that at first they can seem impossible to achieve. He noted that studies show if the stretch goal is audacious, it can spark innovation. These goals

> serve as jolting events that disrupt complacency and promote new ways of thinking," a group of researchers wrote in [the] *Academy of Management Review Business Journal* in 2011. By forcing a substantial elevation in collective aspirations, stretch goals can shift attention to possible new futures and perhaps spark increased energy in the organization. They thus can prompt exploratory learning through experimentation, innovation, broad search, or playfulness. (Duhigg, 2016, p. 127)

To realize a stretch goal, Duhigg suggests breaking the large goal into smaller, manageable goals using the SMART goal format. Locke and Latham (1990) in their research on goal setting used the five-step SMART goal format: (1) specific, (2) measurable, (3) achievable, (4) realistic, and (5) time bound. You feel happy and in control of your life when you have a clear goal you are working toward each day. Becoming a lifelong goal setter is one of the most important disciplines to develop (Tracy, 2010).

Henrietta had a stretch goal—to feed the hungry—a response to her vision and mission. The meals on wheels program she established temporarily met the needs of the hungry. As the numbers of those requesting meals grew, she realized meals on wheels was a temporary fix. While the hospital could not continue to supply meals for all the demands, she had a new stretch goal—establish a center where people could come for a hot meal each weekday.

Looking at that large—seemingly impossible—goal, Henrietta broke the stretch goal into smaller, smarter goals she could realistically achieve. She first established a location that would allow her to cook and serve meals and house the food. This involved several even smarter goals: petitioning the city for support in this endeavor, seeking collaborative partnerships with churches and businesses in the area, requesting food and donations for supplies, and recruiting a team of passionate volunteers to make her initiative viable.

While the city scoffed at the idea, noting that there was no need for this kind of establishment in the area, Henrietta presented her record of meals served within the first three months. Local churches provided data on the outreach program each was doing to meet the needs of the poor. Businesses presented their promise of donations to support the center. After countless meetings, the city succumbed and reluctantly granted permission for this establishment. St. Anthony's Center opened on June 13, 1980.

The stretch goal expanded as Henrietta and her team of volunteers noted the other needs of the people they fed. They needed clothing, household supplies, medical attention, and occasionally temporary shelter. Today, St. Anthony's Center provides a free medical clinic facility, clothing, pre-owned furniture and appliances, shelter during disasters, and retreats for overnight and single-day sessions as well as offering a free hot meal each weekday.

The success of St. Anthony's Center is attributed to its visionary founder and leader, several regular staff members, a corps of more than 100 volunteers, local contributors, a volunteer board of directors, and the ecumenical nature of those who visit and are assisted at St. Anthony's Center. One can only guess at Henrietta's thought process on her journey to her great accomplishment. How did she keep on target, buoyed up, especially when her idea was criticized?

THOUGHTS ARE THINGS: THE VALUE OF SELF-TALK

Self-talk is what you say to yourself either aloud or silently. Dorfman (2000) describes the process of self-talk as a person's response to "situations based on his past experience and the habit of reaction from those experiences. His memory of similar circumstances and their effects on him [provokes] a patterned verbal response. That self-talk is most often a help or a hindrance as he faces a current situation" (p. 214).

As you walk down city streets, a new rage in the past decade has become acceptable practice. Formerly, if you passed someone on the street who was talking out loud you concluded the person had an emotional imbalance. Today, people are tethered to a phone and the talking they do has nothing in common with those they pass on the street.

So talking to yourself may not even seem peculiar in this day and age. Research suggests that self-talk may even support cognitive and emotional development (Neck & Manz, 2010). For example, self-talk is common in fields of performance.

Crowds awaited the performance of the sixteen-year-old gymnast Mary Lou Retton at the 1984 Olympics in Los Angeles. Mary Lou Retton needed a 10, not a 9.95 or even a 9.98, on her last event of the All Around competition at the 1984 Olympic Games to win the gold medal. She did it twice. She scored a perfect 10 on both her vaults. What was she thinking minutes before launching her performance? "Was she thinking 'I'll probably screw up.' Or was she thinking 'I'm gonna nail this perfect 10 just like in practice!' Self-talk is critical" (Kramer, 2014, p. 82).

Self-talk must be grounded in reality and rationality, like Henrietta's was, and not merely in imagination (Dorfman, 2000). The choice of language you use can effectively change the way you think. Positive self-talk will enhance performance while negative self-talk encourages failure. Dorfman coached baseball pitchers to anticipate their performance with enthusiasm and to talk about the task and how to approach it during any competition. He encouraged them to speak in self-affirming, nonjudgmental language using a positive and encouraging tone.

Self-leadership is a process of influencing self to establish self-direction and the motivation needed to perform effectively (Houghton, Wu, Godwin, Neck, & Manz, 2012). Positive self-talk heightens awareness and influence in being and becoming even more optimistic and thus leading self to accomplish set goals and respond to all situations realistically and with eyes wide open. If learning is the acquisition of useful programs, then self-talk can bring about the needed changes in behavior.

Self-talk needs to be geared toward a positive solution to a nagging problem. Whether pitching a baseball or pitching an offer to the city (like Henrietta did), the mission was the problem and the source of its solution.

PROBLEM SOLVERS

Problem solving is the essence of what leaders do. Problem solvers are not a special breed in the population. Everyone is a problem solver.

Dr. Peter Lawrence (1969) wrote a book called *The Peter Principle*. In this humorous presentation, he suggests that in every organization people receive promotions until they reach a level where they are no longer competent to solve the problems of that level. This is where they stop and spend the rest of their careers.

Tracy (2010) suggests that to master problem solving, "you need to develop a formula or method that enables you to deal effectively with almost any problem you face in the face of your career or personal life" (p. 204). He suggests a nine-step method for problem solving:

1. Take time to define the problem carefully.
2. Ask, "Is it really a problem?"
3. Ask, "What else is the problem?"
4. Ask, "How did the problem occur?"
5. Ask, "What are all the possible solutions?"
6. Ask, "What is the best solution at this time?"
7. Make a decision.
8. Assign responsibility.
9. Set a measure for the decision.

The greatest reward you get from problem solving is the satisfaction of solving the problem and the competence you develop in solving bigger problems. You will rise in life to the height of the problem you are capable of solving (Tracy, 2010, p. 206).

WHAT IF THEY DON'T?

Dr. Laurence's *Peter Principle* may best introduce and summarize the notion of what happens when so-called leaders don't lead self. Peter Sutton's foreword in the book describes the frustration of his father who sold furniture and equipment to the U.S. Navy and installed this equipment on ships. He talks about listening to his dad's tirades about government bureaucrats and shipyard managers who insisted that he produce poorly made equipment, how they could barely do their jobs, and how lazy they were. He noted that the Peter principle explained why everyone is doomed to be or become incompetent. Some of the principles of this theory include the following:

1. When you're great at something, you might get rewarded with a promotion . . . into something you're *terrible* at.
2. Once you're promoted to your level of incompetence, you probably *won't* get fired and replaced with someone more competent. Instead, others will work around you.
3. When you're competent, even a dummy can see your *output*. And you're being rewarded for that output. But once you've reached incompetence,

there's little or no output from you. At this point, you'll be judged by your *input*—by how early you arrive at the office, by how cheerful you are, by how you're a good citizen. Rest assured, incompetence is usually not enough to get you fired; only "super-incompetence" is enough to get you fired. And, ironically, "super-competence" will get you fired too, because now you're just making everyone else look bad. As Peter said, the hierarchy must be protected at all costs.
4. Incompetence is perhaps inevitable. So you have to decide whether you want to rush toward the oblivion of Final . . . Or you have to decide whether you want to forestall it as long as you can.
5. If you do decide to rush into a sterile future, . . . you need to exercise the power of "pull"—by attaching yourself to superiors who can help pull you up quickly.
6. If you're smart enough to realize that you don't want to be pulled up the ladder to career limbo, you'll find a happy place where you can be productive and useful, and you'll fight like hell to avoid getting promoted.
7. Because incompetence is inevitable, we shouldn't be trying to fire all the incompetent managers. We'd only replace them with deadwood anyway . . . incompetent people will do the least damage to competent people's productivity if we maintain the benign illusion that they're useful and have a bright future (Asghar, 2014).

EXPEDIENCY VERSUS VISION

What if leaders don't lead self? Let's consider an example of where the leader didn't.

Glenda is an example of expediency versus vision. She was the chair of special education in an urban high school of 2,000 students. She had a passion for special needs students as her own daughter was on the autism spectrum. She knew what services to provide for the seventy-eight classified students in her school, and she even would work with her faculty to discuss the plans that would have the greatest benefits for the students. That was in the beginning. Circumstances change and so did Glenda.

Glenda was not present totally even when she was at school. She often came late to school, where she hid in her office and spent blocks of time on the phone. She taught two classes each day, but often the students were allowed to talk with each other or text friends if they completed work early—which was almost daily.

Glenda started a small business running a nursery school. Each morning before coming to the high school, she would spend time checking in at the nursery school. This was one reason she was often late. As soon as her last class was finished, she was out the door. Clearly, her passion was the nursery school while the high school paid her a second salary.

Glenda had a vision for the nursery school, and this vision was always before her. And while that vision was commendable, it did not match the needs of the high school students and staff. Her time was so divided that even when she was at the high school her thoughts were elsewhere.

Glenda would make arrangements for meetings and conferences around a schedule in her own best interest. Expediency became a way of operating while she was at the high school. She became less involved with the needs of the individual students and staff and established patterns of behavior that suited her. Her self-talk walked her through each day justifying why her decisions were acceptable.

As Tracy (2010) noted in his insights on problem solvers, you become what you think. In Glenda's mind, her commitment to the nursery school was admirable. After all, she was holding down two jobs and this had to be best for her family. But meanwhile Glenda failed to lead herself in recognizing her real vision and mission and she lacked the courage to face the reality of moving from good to great.

Glenda was doing good work. But she could not lead herself to do the right work at the right time. She used excuses that supported the least resistance approach with her high school staff to make choices for the students that were minimally supportive and required the least amount of involvement on her part. In more than one case, she did not require the staff to complete the service program that was required for the students.

Glenda is an example of the 80–20 principle on the wrong side of the equation. She would spend 80 percent of her time covering for herself, leading herself to make excuses for what she did not do, ignoring the vision and mission right before her because her goals were not the goals of the organization. Growing into leadership was not possible for Glenda in this situation. She would need to decide if she would align her own vision and mission to lead herself. She needed skills to lead herself to serve the mission.

REFERENCES

Asghar, R. (2014, August 14). Incompetence rains, er, reigns: What the Peter Principle means today. Forbes. Retrieved from http://www.forbes.com/sites/robasghar/2014/08/14/incompetence-rains-er-reigns-what-the-peter-principle-means-today/#7cceaa09631b

Bambrick-Santoyo, P. (2012). *Leveraging leadership: A practical guide to building exceptional schools.* San Francisco, CA: Jossey-Bass.

Covey, S. R. (1989). *The 7 habits of highly effective people.* New York, NY: Free Press.

Dorfman, H. A. (2000). *The mental ABC's of pitching: A handbook for performance enhancement*. Lanham, MD: Diamond Communications.

Drucker, P. F. (2008). *Managing oneself*. Boston, MA: Harvard Business Review Press.

Duhigg, C. (2016). *Smarter, faster, better: The secrets of being productive in life and business*. New York, NY: Random House.

Houghton, J. D., Wu, J., Godwin, J. L., Neck, C. P., & Manz, C. C. (2012). Effective stress management: A model of emotional intelligence, self-leadership, and student stress coping. *Journal of Management Education* 36(2), 220–238.

Jones, L. B. (1996). *The path: Creating your mission statement for work and for life*. New York, NY: Hyperion.

Kramer, D. (2014). *Entering the real world: Timeless ideas not learned in school*. Lanham, MD: Rowman & Littlefield.

Locke, E. A., & Latham, G. P. (1990). *A theory of goal setting and task performance*. Englewood Cliffs, NJ: Prentice Hall.

Mayo, A. J., & Nohria, N. (2005). *In their time: The greatest business leaders of the twentieth century*. Boston, MA: Harvard Business Review.

Neck, C. P., & Manz, C. C. (2010). *Mastering self-leadership: Empowering yourself for personal excellence*, 5th ed. Upper Saddle River, NJ: Prentice Hall.

Peter, L. J., & Hull, R. (1969). *The Peter principle*. New York, NY: W. Morrow.

Ryan, J. (2009, July 29). Leadership success always starts with vision. *Forbes*. Retrieved from http://www.forbes.com/2009/07/29/personal-success-vision-leadership-managing-ccl.html

Tracy, B. (2010). *No excuses! The power of self-discipline*. New York, NY: MJF Books.

Chapter 5

If You Always Succeed, You Are Overqualified

> *A leader will find it difficult to articulate a coherent vision unless it expresses his core values, his basic identity. One must first embark on the formidable journey of self-discovery in order to create a vision with authentic soul.*
>
> —Mihaly Csikszentmihalyi

Exhibiting leadership in the face of difficulty requires the skill of recognizing the problem before dealing with its personal impact or reaction to the problem. The skill of presenting a solution requires personal mastery over the impulse to defend oneself. The skill of using conflict to promote consensus requires the skill of analyzing the values that "bookend" the conflict continuum.

This chapter identifies skills to lead self—the one Glenda needs (see chapter 4). These skills include writing and living by personal mission and vision, examining and prioritizing the 168 hours found in each week, taking steps to promote the will to learn, cultivating positive self-talk, and using the six steps of the LEADER model for problem solving.

SEEING THE VISION AND LIVING THE MISSION

Every leader has a vision and the mission to bring the vision to reality. Vision and mission statements are often found in corporations:

> Ford's vision statement is *"people working together as a lean, global enterprise for automotive leadership."* Ford's mission statement is *"One Team. One Plan. One Goal."*
>
> Google's vision statement is *"to provide access to the world's information in one click."* Google's mission statement is *"to organize the world's information and make it universally accessible and useful."*

Wendy's vision statement is *"to be the quality leader in everything we do."* Wendy's mission statement is *"to deliver superior quality products and services for our customers and communities through leadership, innovation and partnerships."* (Panmore Institute, 2016)

Personal vision and mission statements are important. If you do not know who you are and what you stand for, or where you want to be, you cannot lead yourself, or others, or organizations.

Vision statements envision the ideal future. They answer the following questions: Where do I want to be? What is the optimal future state? Vision statements are more emotional, and they help you define your core values. Vision statements are more descriptive of the preferred future.

Mission statements are more present oriented to move toward the future. They answer the following question: What do you want now and how will you achieve it? They describe what you want to achieve in life but in a more specific and measurable way. Laurie Beth Jones (1996) in *The Path* suggests that mission statements are a single sentence long, easily understood by a twelve-year-old, and are able to be recited from memory even at gunpoint.

Developing personal vision and mission statements is a highly introspective task. One does not need to precede the other so you can develop a mission statement and then a vision statement, or vice versa.

Books have been written on developing vision and mission statements. While there are many examples for formulating vision and mission statements, in this text we will examine formats suggested by Covey (1989) and Jones (1996).

DEVELOPING A PERSONAL VISION STATEMENT

A vision statement is your ideal. The statement describes who you are, what you will accomplish, and what difference this has made in the world. Jones (1996) states the following as key elements in a vision statement:

1. It is written down.
2. It is written in present tense, as if it has already been accomplished.
3. It covers a variety of activities and time frames.
4. It is filled with descriptive details that anchor it to reality. (pp. 73–74)

Personal vision statements reveal your positive prophecies about yourself as well as your unique selling points. Effective vision statements reflect how your passion is your power.

Anthony Cioffi (2016) expressed his vision in this way in his résumé when he applied to be Region 1 governor official nominee for the American Society of Civil Engineers:

> As an ASCE Region 1 Governor, I will be an advocate and ambassador for the Civil Engineering profession and the American Society of Civil Engineers. Through a dedicated commitment to excellence, I will strive to advance the profession and will continually represent our profession in a positive light. I will respect others and will lead by example.

Other vision statements are more detailed. Elena Aguilar (2012), a transformational leadership coach, wrote this as her vision statement:

> I coach to heal and transform the world. I coach teachers and leaders to discover ways of working and being that are joyful and rewarding, that bring communities together, and that result in positive outcomes for children. I coach people to find their own power and to empower others so that we can transform our education system, our society, and our world.

A personal vision statement inspires you. It motivates you with possibilities and promises. It paints a future of hope.

MAPPING YOUR MISSION

Mission statements are more prevalent and available than vision statements. The mission describes the path you take in life. It focuses on what you want to be, what you want to do, and the values and principles upon which being and doing are based (Covey, 1989). Every life decision is made based on your mission and how you make use of your time, talent, and energy.

Stephen Covey (1989) suggests that writing a mission statement begins with identifying the principles that guide you in all aspects of your life. Which principles are core in your life? Do you believe and work toward excellence? Is truth how you shape your response to people and circumstances? How do you regard challenge?

He also suggests that you describe in detail your current roles. No one is just pigeonholed into one role. Reflection on those roles and how those roles interrelate give a clearer idea of mission. Your role is not just your career (guidance counselor), although that may be one of your roles. You may also be parent, child, scholar, neighbor, and church member. Each role has goals, and these goals need to be considered in developing your mission.

Stephen Covey developed a workbook as a brief overview of his seven habits to effective leadership. This workbook also provides a six-step process to begin writing a personal mission statement. This detailed process allows you to discover as well as create your personal mission statement. Using a combination of Senge's *The Fifth Discipline* and Covey's *7 Habits of Highly Effective People*, the Rochester School District created a mission statement retreat program that is available online for following these steps. The six-step process and the included worksheets help identify core principles and values in a reflective manner in creating at least a first draft of a personal mission (see https://www.jmu.edu/osarp/civiclearning/files/mission-creation-Senge-Covey.pdf).

Jones (1996) gives a more simplified version for developing a mission statement. She suggests that you generate a list of verbs that excite you and after generating the list that you choose the three that most excite you, for example, *teach, create, engage, inspire.*

Next, determine and write what you stand for—your principles, values, core, causes, reason for being (e.g., excellence, equity, freedom, justice). Then list whom you will help—the cause, entity, organization. This is the template she uses:

My mission is to:

_____, _____, and _____
[Your three verbs]

_____
[Your core value or values]
to, for, with, or through

_____.
[the group/cause which most moves/excites you]

Jones (1996, p. 63)

A sample mission statement based on the template is as follows: *My mission is to teach, engage, and inspire the next generation of educators to embrace teaching and learning for urban adolescents.*

The very act of developing a personal mission statement is an exercise in building a skill for leading self. The personal mission statement is not just the exercise but includes regular review of the choices to live the mission. The mission is made obvious in all aspects of life, including family, professional, personal, academic, social, religious, and, yes, even your hidden life.

YOU HAVE THE SAME 168 HOURS

No matter how you do the math, you still have 168 hours a week allocated to you. The question remains how you choose to use those hours.

Leading self requires a careful examination of the skill needed for how time is used.

Managing time, people, paper, and money is a clear indication of the real leader. However, with these four variables, only one is immutable and unchangeable and that is time. Each hour is 60 minutes, each day is 24 hours, and each week is 168 hours. When you take time to track how you use those hours, you have a clearer indication of how you are leading yourself.

As we consider the commonly held time frames, general agreement is found that the work week involves 40 hours and recommended sleep of 8 hours a day totals 56 hours a week. That total of 96 hours is where most of our time is spent each week. But that still leaves us with 72 other hours. Some of that time is spent with eating and preparing to eat as well as cleaning up after eating. Hopefully, some time is spent each day with some form of exercising. Connecting with others beyond the workplace is also a regular part of the day. But where do all those hours go?

Laura Vanderkam (2010) in her book *168 Hours: You Have More Time than You Think* interviewed dozens of happy and successful people, and she found that their allocation of time is different from what most people do. She tells how these people set priorities and use them as their goals in their planning. In looking at the coming day, they use the skills to allocate the needed time to accomplish these priorities.

Making time for the important things in life requires the discipline and skill to make and keep a calendar. Vanderkam suggests spending a week recording how you currently spend your time. Most weeks are typical weeks (with the exception of vacations or sick leave), so almost any week will work. The discipline to keep track of how you use time can be supported by Vanderkam's online spreadsheet at My168Hours.com (http://laura vanderkam.com/books/168-hours/manage-your-time/).

Examining how you spend your 168 hours can provide insights into determining a priority by the amount of time dedicated to a task. Even with time at work, few people truly work a 40-hour week. During the week you spend examining your own use of time, break your workday into smaller tasks such as responding to email, making phone calls, surfing the Internet, and attending required meetings, self-selected meetings, and spontaneous meetings. Then ask yourself what your job really is and figure out how much time you allocate to the important activities of your job.

Once you have an idea of how you currently allocate your time, begin to use the calendar to prioritize your time. Each week, you need to determine goals and how those goals contribute to roles. Block out times in the week for you to accomplish those goals. This kind of planning supports your own vision and mission as you take the roles you identified there; now prioritize your time throughout the week.

Table 5.1. Covey Calendar Template

The Weekly Schedule		Sunday	Monday	Tuesday	Wednesday	Thursday	Friday	Saturday
Roles	Goals	Today's Priorities						
Sharpen the Saw		Appointments/Commitments						
		8	8	8	8	8	8	8
		9	9	9	9	9	9	9
		10	10	10	10	10	10	10
		11	11	11	11	11	11	11
Physical		12	12	12	12	12	12	12
		1	1	1	1	1	1	1
		2	2	2	2	2	2	2
Mental		3	3	3	3	3	3	3
		4	4	4	4	4	4	4
		5	5	5	5	5	5	5
Spiritual		6	6	6	6	6	6	6
		7	7	7	7	7	7	7
		8	8	8	8	8	8	8
Social/ emotional		Evening	Evening	Evening	Evening	Evening	Evening	Evening

Based on Covey (1989) *The 7 Habits of Highly Effective People.*

Reflecting on how time is used provides insights for priorities. To lead self, a clear indication of priorities and designated times to address the priorities contributes to a balanced personal life. Without this awareness, balance does not exist and leading self does not happen.

Both Vanderkam (2010) and Covey (1989) advocate creating a weekly calendar. Leading self requires the discipline of planning your time as it relates to your roles and goals. The weekly calendar becomes a reference point for what was planned and then reconciling the plan with reality. See table 5.1 for a sample template for planning a week.

LEADERS OF THEIR OWN LEARNING

How common it is for those in education to develop learning plans with and for students. Explanations for why students should have learning plans include having students take more responsibility for their own learning, having them set goals and plans to accomplish goals, and having them use their time more productively. These plans can motivate students to challenge themselves academically and in other areas. These plans help the educator learn students' interests and skills. If plans are critical for students, how much more is a learning plan essential for leaders?

Tracy (2010) tells the story of Bob Barton, who started at a large sales company in his early twenties. He started at the bottom and associated with colleagues in the same rankings. Within the first few months, he noticed that top executives associated with each other. They did not spend time with underlings. They spent their time differently—arriving early, following written plans for the day, making telephone calls and appointments to make the sales.

Bob decided to follow the patterns of behavior he was observing and created a personal plan to become one of the top executives. Bob dressed like the executives. He arrived early and started making calls by 8:30. He asked one of the executives to recommend a book that would help him learn how to develop his skills. He immediately bought the book and followed the suggestions therein. He consulted with another executive to find out how he scheduled his day. The shared time management techniques were put to immediate use. Bob continued to consult the top executives, follow their advice, and moved up to one of the top salespersons' positions within six months.

Bob did something that most people do not. He sought the advice of successful people and he followed their advice. Seek to learn from the best.

Develop your learning by investing in yourself. Tracy (2010) found that if you invest 3 percent of your earnings back into yourself that seems to be a magic number for lifelong learning—more mathematical leadership! If you are earning $50,000 a year, take 3 percent of that total ($1,500) and use that to improve yourself. Invest in books to read, seminars to attend, courses to take. Keep raising the bar. With successive increases in salary, maintain the 3 percent formula in increasing your personal investment.

As you invest 3 percent of your money to improve your learning, invest 3 percent of your time to improve yourself. Carve out time to read daily. Spend at least one hour each day reading professionally to grow in your field. While some believe top performers are in that category because of their talents, Geoffrey Colvin (2010) found that research indicates that great performance is a result of great and ongoing practice. Most people do their jobs in the first few years and from there they coast.

One superintendent referred to the laminated lesson plans teachers had—they created the plan during their first year of teaching and then used the plan every year thereafter—one year's experience countless times. One secretary felt the scourge of a college professor. When she ordered his textbook, she ordered the latest version. When he saw the new version he required her to send the books back and get his old version to match his PowerPoint slides—laminated lesson plans.

The leader who stops learning stops performing. To make the move from average to good and good to great, invest in yourself. A greater investment—3 percent, 4 percent, 5 percent, or more—will get you to the top of your game in leading self.

SELF-TALK—THE SIXTH S

Leaders talk to themselves. The quality of those conversations contribute to leading self. A source for applying the skills needed to lead self might be found in the Japanese guide to productivity and effectiveness called the 5S (https://www.kaizen.com/knowledge-center/what-is-5s.html.) based on five Japanese words that begin with S. Each word represents a simple action that requires self-discipline and consistent action. These five actions can help leaders develop skills for leading self that influence others.

During the era immediately following World War II, Japan—with a major renovation to accomplish—developed the 5S principles as part of the quality movement. The goal was to eliminate any obstacles to efficient production. The 5Ss are Japanese words that have been translated loosely in English to *sort, systematize or simplify, sweep, sanitize or standardize,* and *self-discipline* (Becker, 2001).

The 5S technique has been practiced in Japan ever since. An ideal work environment is more often a dream than a reality. This ideal means the environment works efficiently 100 percent of the time and in 100 percent of the ways. Most practitioners of the 5Ss consider the process useful for not only improving the physical environment but also strengthening thinking processes.

To sort is to eliminate anything that is unusable in the situation or to return to storage something that has been used. Systematizing or simplifying involves designating a place for everything and where access is easy. Sweep indicates keeping the place clean. Standardizing or sanitizing means establishing visual controls and guidelines for keeping order that becomes habitual. Self-discipline, the fifth S, is the commitment to the first 4Ss as a way of life (Ho, 1991).

While this whole process refers to the workplace, the elements are applicable and recommended for leading self. Creating a total quality management system to lead self requires the discipline and skills of each of the five components.

To implement the 5Ss, a *sixth S*—self-talk—is a necessary skill to lead self. Seligman (1991) in his book *Learned Optimism* suggests that a most significant finding in psychology in the last twenty years is that individuals can choose the way they think. As noted in the previous chapter, self-talk is what we tell ourselves. Various studies in different fields support the relationship between constructive self-talk and performance (Neck & Manz, 1992).

One aspect of self-talk for consideration is opportunity thinking versus obstacle thinking. Opportunity thinking involves a pattern of thoughts that focuses on opportunities, worthwhile challenges, and constructive ways of dealing with challenging situations. Obstacle thinking, on the other hand, involves a focus on the negative aspects (the obstacles) involved in challenging situations—for example, reasons to give up and retreat from a problem (Neck & Manz, 1992).

Another way to develop constructive self-talk is through consideration of "trial and successes." Sullivan (1953) suggests that learning occurs through trial and success rather than through trial and error, which better supports constructive thinking. An individual learns by focusing on his or her successes rather than failures.

Seligman (1991) argued that when confronted by a bad situation, optimists "perceive it as a challenge and try harder whereas pessimists believe bad events will last a long time and will undermine everything they do" (pp. 4–5). Bandura's work with self-efficacy suggests that past performance is the strongest contributor to perceived self-efficacy. The level of perceived self-efficacy has been found to affect the amount of effort expended and the degree of persistence, of which both are significantly related to performance (Bandura, 1986). Beliefs, internal dialogues, mental imagery, and thought patterns are the cognitive strategies and skills that manage thinking and subsequently improve performance.

Max made his first presentation to his board members early in the financial year. He was prepared for his presentation—having selected three major areas of recent successes in the business and identifying the two areas he and the corporate staff agreed to be the area of improvement for the year. As most of the board members were strangers to him, he quickly became flustered in his presentation as he could remember neither the name of the board president nor the names of the members. With a focus on remembering their names, he failed to present all three areas of success and placed a greater emphasis on areas of improvement. Max felt that this first meeting set a tone of negativity rather than the upbeat tone he wanted to communicate.

Identifying the dysfunction and then altering the thoughts that occur to be more rational in nature can be accomplished through self-talk. Max could challenge his thoughts of himself as a complete failure and revise his beliefs regarding himself using constructive self-talk, such as "I've made successful presentations before; I will learn from this mistake. It's not the end of the world; I will do better next time" (Neck & Manz, 1992). Change the thinking by changing the self-talk. Lead self by establishing patterns of opportunity thinking.

LEADER: SIX STEPS IN ADDRESSING PROBLEMS

All aspects of life involve opportunities and challenges. A SWOT analysis is common in the industry and just as important in leading self. Strengths and weaknesses are often internal issues that need attention while opportunities and threats are external to the individual. But all four elements impact how you develop skills to lead yourself.

The core components of any group are the individuals who make up the group. To use SWOT analysis effectively within the group requires that each member use the SWOT analysis individually. Each individual has to have a self-learning process to lead self. Vanderkam (2010) proposes that years of experience without years of improving are fruitless. The LEADER model is one way to engage in leading self through a systematic process in problem solving. The process includes six steps (see figure 5.1)

This model was first introduced to students and staff of a PK-grade 8 school as a vehicle to help students solve their own problems. The staff had noted that students easily relegated their "problems" to an adult whom they expected would "fix the problem." These problems included not having a pencil, forgetting homework, or not having anything to do on the playground during recess. Teachers recognized that as long as staff members "solved" these problems, students would be content with taking less responsibility for their own development (Jacobs & Cooper, 2016). The teachers collectively used the model to teach problem-solving skills, particularly as they related to real life and everyday problems in school.

This easy-to-remember problem-solving format is as effective for individuals who wish to assume personal responsibility as it is for addressing more complex issues. Often, pathways to anywhere are scattered with excuses, and

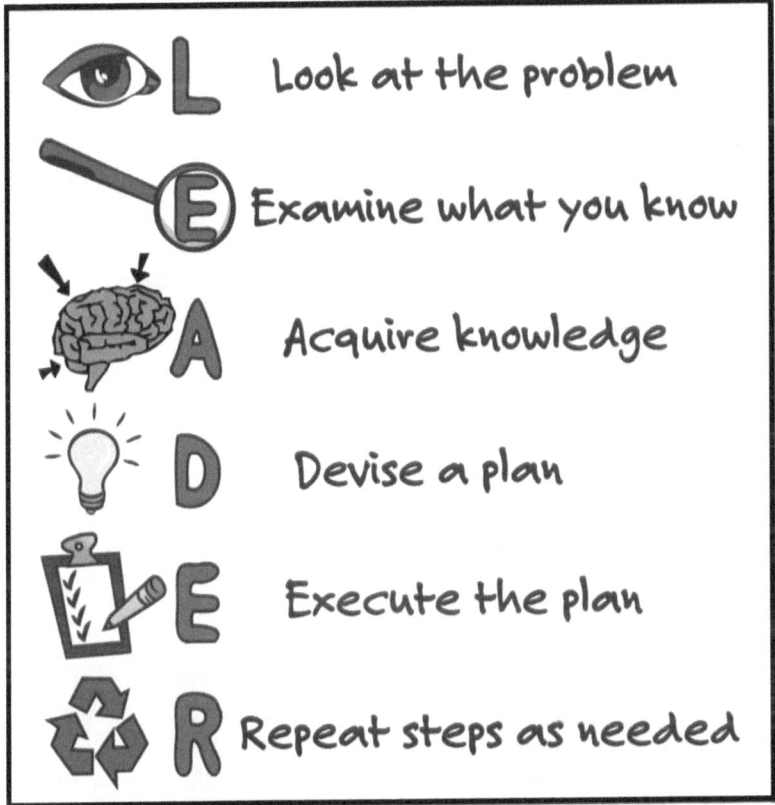

Figure 5.1. The LEADER Model for Problem Solving. Original Artwork by Melissa Rossiter. Graphic Design by Jordyn Jacobs

the main purpose of excuses is to deflect criticism. Making excuses precludes the need to learn to correct mistakes or address problems that may or may not be apparent. Problems can be seen as pitfalls or possibilities. Leading self requires the ability to develop a format for addressing personal and corporate problems, issues, and challenges. Seeing a problem is one thing; taking steps to solve the problem is a critical skill for leading self. Chapter 13 describes the six steps of this process in greater detail.

WHAT IF THEY DON'T?

Lacking the basics skills for leading self leads to disaster. Facing oneself requires an honesty and courage that allows one to see a realistic picture. People do not always see themselves realistically. Judging oneself often takes a different approach from judging others. In judging other people, the approach is often based on the actions others have taken.

The house mortgage that never happened was because the mortgage company did not file the paperwork with the bank in a timely fashion. The job termination was due to the company's lack of profit share. The cost of plane reservations escalated because the vacation was planned at a peak vacation time. These reasons are easy to justify—someone did not do what should have been done.

Looking in the mirror, that someone could be one's self! However, the reflection is not always based on the action but rather on the perceived intention of the action. When one does not see clearly, "good intentions" can be used as the excuse for leading self down the wrong path.

Karl was the associate director of business technology. His main role was assuring effective technological communication within the workplace. He reported to Stephan—generally in monthly reports based on the responses to executed tickets generated when employees identified a problem.

With the start of the new fiscal year, a new communication strategy training program was unfolding for all current employees. Karl created a training calendar and shared designated training sessions with each department. After the first round of training sessions, complaints surfaced regarding the program. The first department that received the training identified issues with the implementation of the social media aspect of the program. Karl responded that the issue was being considered. The departments involved in the second round of training identified problems with the email server. By the third round of training, Karl faced another department complaining about the speed needed to send documents to potential clients. Karl's response was basically the same each time: the problem was being addressed.

As employees continued to identify issues with the new program, Stephan was contacted by several department heads. When Karl was questioned about the program, Karl told Stephan that the employees needed more time to get used to the program. Karl indicated that few tickets for resolving issues were received because the problems were experienced only by a few employees. Karl contacted all department heads and informed them that tickets would no longer be used to report issues with the new program.

As training sessions continued, more issues with the new program surfaced. Karl was adamant about not using tickets to report issues—until Stephan called for a meeting with Karl and department heads. Where was the breakdown in Karl's ability to lead self in this situation?

Karl lacked a vision for the role he played in this company. He relied on preventing top management from hearing about any issues within his purview. The selection of the new program was based on an efficiency model—it was cheaper and saving money would be regarded favorably from top ranks. Karl did not enhance his own learning by participating in the available training sessions. Karl refused to look at the real problem or take the necessary steps to resolve issues.

While leaders may have a position, there is no guarantee they are leading. In Karl's case, the skills to lead self—a vision, learning to learn, and problem solving—were underdeveloped. Karl focused on approval from above while ignoring his own development as a leader.

Leaders find it difficult to articulate a vision unless it expresses their core values. The journey within—leading self—must be the first step in all journeys of leadership.

REFERENCES

Aguilar, E. (2012, June 1). Teachers, what's your vision? Edutopia. Retrieved from http://www.edutopia.org/blog/teacher-vision-mission-elena-aguilar

Bandura, A. (1986). *Social foundations of thought and action: A social cognitive theory*. Englewood Cliffs, NJ: Prentice-Hall.

Becker, J. E. (2001). Implementing 5S: To promote safety & housekeeping. *Professional Safety* 46(8), 29.

Cioffi, A. (2016). Anthony L. Cioffic, P.E., M.ASCE Region 1 Governor Official Nominee. ASCE. Retrieved from http://www.asce.org/templates/person-candidate-detail.aspx?id=14934#vision

Colvin, G. (2010). *Talent is overrated: What really separates world-class performers from everybody else*. New York, NY: Penguin Group.

Covey, S. R. (1989). *The 7 habits of highly effective people*. New York, NY: Free Press.

Ho, S. K. (1991). TQM and change management via 5S. Retrieved from http://www.saferpak.com/fives_art7.htm

Jacobs, S. M. A., & Cooper, B. S. (2016). *Action research in the classroom: Helping teachers assess and improve their work*. Lanham, MD: Rowman & Littlefield.

Jones, L. B. (1996). *The path: Creating your mission statement for work and for life*. New York, NY: Hyperion.

Neck, C. P., & Manz, C. C. (1992). Thought self-leadership: The influence of self-talk and mental imagery on performance. *Journal of Organizational Behavior* 13(7), 681–699.

Panmore Institute. (2016). Vision and mission statements. Retrieved from http://panmore.com/tag/vision-and-mission-statements

Seligman, M. E. P. (1991). *Learned optimism: How to change your mind and your life*. New York: Alfred A. Knopf.

Sullivan, H. S. (1953). *The interpersonal theory of psychiatry*. New York: W. W. Norton & Company.

Tracy, B. (2010). *No excuses! The power of self-discipline*. New York, NY: MJF Books.

Vanderkam, L. (2010). *168 Hours: You have more time than you think*. New York, NY: Penguin Group.

Chapter 6

All Change Begins with a Change of Mind

All things are created twice: There's a mental or first creation, and a physical or second creation to all things.

—Stephen Covey

Because all change begins with a change of mind, there are dispositions of mind and heart that have to be developed to use knowledge and skill effectively. These dispositions are mental post-it notes made through self-talk, qualities of the mind and heart that influence our responses. Leaders need to develop the sense that power is not a four-letter word, that victimhood is optional, that thoughts are things, and that change is inevitable but growth is a choice. This chapter examines the dispositions for leading self.

COURAGE: THE FUNDAMENTAL DISPOSITION

Johanna Mansfield Sullivan, the oldest child of Thomas and Alice Sullivan, was born in Feeding Hills, Agawam, Massachusetts, in 1866, just a decade after the Civil War. Her parents were illiterate, unskilled immigrants who came to the United States from Ireland during the Great Famine.

When Johanna was about five years old, she contracted a serious eye infection that left her nearly blind and afflicted with repeated, intense, painful infections. Because of this eye condition, she had no skills in reading or writing and could not perform basic needed skills such as sewing.

When she was eight years old, her mother died. Her father abandoned Johanna and her younger brother Jimmie two years later, fearing he could not care for them. The siblings were taken to an almshouse, where her brother died just two or three months after arriving. Johanna was left alone. She remained at the almshouse for about four years after Jimmie's death. During that time, she had a series of eye operations that offered temporary relief but ultimately proved ineffective.

During her stay at the almshouse, another resident told Johanna about schools for the blind. During an inspection of the almshouse in 1880, Johanna convinced the inspector to send her to the Perkins School for the Blind. She began her studies there later that year.

Johanna experienced great challenges during her first years at Perkins. Because of her rough mannerisms, others did not easily accept her at the school. Eventually, she made good connections with a few of the teachers and gradually learned to read and write and the manners to be socially acceptable. While at the school, she learned and mastered the manual alphabet, a finger-spelling alphabet and numerical system often used in deaf education. During her stay at Perkins, she underwent a series of eye operations resulting in better eye sight. At the age of twenty, Johanna graduated as the valedictorian of her class.

She stated: "Fellow-graduates: duty bids us go forth into active life. Let us go cheerfully, hopefully, and earnestly, and set ourselves to find our especial part. When we have found it, willingly and faithfully perform it" (McGinnity, Seymour-Ford, & Andries, 2004). And so she did.

Within a year of her graduation, she became the teacher of a blind and deaf seven-year-old named Helen. It was the beginning of a forty-nine-year relationship that evolved from teacher, to governess, and then friend. Johanna, better known as Annie Sullivan, spent the rest of her life as the teacher and companion of Helen Keller, who herself was acclaimed as a blind and deaf author, political activist, and lecturer (Royal National Institute of Blind People, 2014).

More than 100 years later, a nationwide online poll commissioned by the nonprofit research group Research! America found that blindness is what many Americans fear most. The top concerns with vision loss were the quality of life and loss of independence (Preidt, 2016). In his banquet address at the Annual Convention of the National Federation of the Blind, Mark Riccobono (2016) talked about fear and how, "if we resolve ourselves to face our fears, respect the power within those fears, and turn that power into action, we can take control of our own destiny, diminish the negative fears of others, and raise our expectations."

By all expectations, Annie Sullivan should not have been a successful person. What made Annie exceptional was her courage. To have courage is to have heart. *Courage* comes from the Latin *cor*, meaning heart. To have courage is to act bravely in spite of the existence of fear (Dorfman, 2000).

No one would deny the necessity of courage for all leaders, although seldom is this disposition discussed in conversations about educational leadership. Not a day goes by that a leader is not challenged to face the courage of his or her convictions. Sandy Hook Elementary School is a prime example, where six staff members gave their lives for children. While this type of courage is not often demanded, daily acts of courage are.

Eric, a seventh grader, frequently displayed acts of anger. He would pound his fists into walls, trees, and concrete fittings. He would storm around the gym breathing heavily and talking to himself. While he never injured himself or threatened others, Ms. Doran, the principal of a small private school, recognized these behaviors as indicators of a troubled youth. Eric needed help; despite frequent conversations with both parents, Ms. Doran found that they insisted that Eric had things under control.

Ms. Doran was not satisfied with the parents' explanation. While she considered the alternative action the parents may take (transferring Eric out of the school), she chose to stand by the courage of her conviction that she had to address the issue for Eric's sake. She met again with the parents and shared her ongoing concerns. Eric's mother was adamant that he was fine and did not need any help. His father was more silent, although not outwardly supportive of Ms. Doran's concern. Because this was a private school, Ms. Doran took a courageous next step: she told Eric's parents that in order for him to continue as a student at the school, he had to be enrolled in a program for counseling.

Erik's mother stormed out of the meeting. His father responded that they would get back to her regarding their decision. The following day, they requested a transfer for Eric.

As a result, Ms. Doran was uncertain about Eric's future and remained greatly concerned about his emotional well-being. The parents never contacted the principal again. But two years later, when Eric was in high school, he stopped by the school to speak with Ms. Doran. He thanked her for the actions she took. He explained that he knew he needed help and after his parents told him he was not returning to the school, he insisted on getting the help he knew he needed. Eric had been in therapy for the past two years, and he said that he finally understood his own anger issues. If Ms. Doran had not taken those drastic, courageous steps, he was unsure if he would be alive today.

Courage is only one of the many dispositions needed to lead self. Two types of courage must be practiced: the courage that takes action, as did Ms. Doran, and the courage to persevere.

Bill Fallon, a successful real estate broker and a professional skier, had to find the courage to persevere in the midst of personal tragedy. In 1990, he finally learned what caused the headaches he experienced since childhood—a brain tumor. He would face more than fifty hours of experimental brain surgery and would have to learn how to walk, read, ski, and live again. He discovered how strength in his family and focusing on a goal to return to skiing helped with his physical and psychological healing and building his life once again. Bill Fallon found the courage to persevere.

MISSION-DRIVEN DISPOSITIONS

It is no secret that today's schools, businesses, and health-related corporations face serious and mounting challenges. Neither is it a secret that passionate, visionary, data-informed organizational leaders are essential if these organizations are going to successfully meet these challenges and overcome them and thrive (Holter & Frabutt, 2012).

Prentice Mulford, considered by some as among the strangest of men, is credited as one of the earliest pioneers in new-thought teaching. Mulford envisioned the airplane and the radio—before they came into being. He believed that thoughts were things. His learning was not book knowledge but rather accrued through his observations and reflections nourished by his contact with nature. Some regarded his thoughts as mere dreams while others regarded his thoughts as priceless truths. Mulford (1908) had his own insights into the positive and negative visions of self.

> THERE belongs to every human being a higher self and a lower self—a self or mind of the spirit which has been growing for ages, and a self of the body, which is but a thing of yesterday. The higher self is full of prompting idea, suggestion and aspiration. This it receives of the Supreme Power. All this the lower or animal self regards as wild and visionary. The higher self argues possibilities and power for us greater than men and women now possess and enjoy. The lower self says we can only live and exist as men and women have lived and existed before us. The higher self craves freedom from the cumbrousness, the limitations, the pains and disabilities of the body. The lower self says that we are born to them, born to ill, born to suffer, and must suffer as have so many before us. The higher self wants a standard for right and wrong of its own. The lower self says we must accept a standard made for us by others—by general and long-held opinion, belief and prejudice. "To thine own self be true" is an oft-uttered adage. But to which self? The higher or lower? (p. 4)

Leading self requires dispositions that get at who you are and what is at the core of your being. The story of the three bricklayers has been around for years. The author remains unknown. The story unfolds like this: Once upon a time, there were three bricklayers. Each was asked the same question: "What are you doing?" The first bricklayer responded: "I'm laying bricks." The second bricklayer responded: "I'm putting up a wall." The third brick layer responded: "I'm building a cathedral."

What draws you, drives you, pushes you, pulls you? You are the only one who can answer these questions. Your answers indicate the extent of your ability to lead self on a path that lays bricks or builds a cathedral.

Table 6.1 shows a disposition inventory based on the Individual Leadership Self-Assessment (ILSA) instrument. This inventory has been used in

Table 6.1. Dispositions Section of the ILSA

Perceptions of Self	1	2	3	4	5	6	7
I identify positively with others, even those who are different from me.							
I always try to see the other person's point of view.							
I display a generally positive attitude toward life and work.							
I am accepting of others whose ideas and opinions differ from mine.							
I accept constructive criticism.							
I display a general belief that all people are valuable, able, and worthy.							

Perceptions of Others	1	2	3	4	5	6	7
I collaborate positively with others.							
I share responsibility with others.							
I find positive things about almost everyone I meet.							
I share credit for accomplishments with others.							

Perceptions of Purpose	1	2	3	4	5	6	7
I see the big picture in most situations.							
I treat everyone equitably and fairly.							
I see work in the larger context of a person's life.							
I avoid being sidetracked by trivia or petty issues.							
I am committed to lifelong learning for myself and others.							

Frame of Reference	1	2	3	4	5	6	7
My primary focus is on the success of the people with whom I interact.							
I balance work and life.							
I build and maintain positive relationships with colleagues.							
I build and maintain positive relationships with clients.							
I focus on the human aspects (rather than things) in most situations.							

Rating Scale Instructions for the ILSA Instructions:

Choose the number that best matches your current perception of the trait/characteristic or skill indicated on this survey.

1—I do not exhibit this trait/characteristic/skill/disposition
2—I infrequently exhibit this trait/characteristic/skill/disposition
3—I occasionally exhibit this trait/characteristic/skill/disposition
4—I usually exhibit this trait/characteristic/skill/disposition
5—I frequently exhibit this trait/characteristic/skill/disposition
6—I frequently exhibit this trait/characteristic/skill, and many other people have told me that I exhibit this trait/characteristic/skill/disposition
7—I frequently exhibit this trait/characteristic/skill, and most other people have told me that I exhibit this trait/characteristic/skill/disposition

http://files.eric.ed.gov/fulltext/EJ1024114.pdf

doctoral programs in Northern Kentucky University to ascertain the development of dispositions related to developing leadership (Allen, Wasicsko, & Chirichello, 2014).

Users are invited to receive feedback on their own leadership by completing the Individual Leadership Self-Assessment at http://leaderdispositions.org/. The site recommends that each user identify ten or more critical friends who will receive the same survey to respond about the user's leadership dispositions. The user will receive a graph comparing the user's perception to the perceptions of the critical friends. Use of the inventory is free.

Identifying your own dispositions toward self, others, life purposes, and frames of reference provides reflective insights. Inviting others who have served with you in your leadership positions—critical friends, colleagues, supervisors, to give feedback as they perceive you—adds another dimension to leading self. Compare your perceptions with these others and determine the leadership dispositions you have and those you want to cultivate.

DISPOSED TO HAPPINESS

Leading self can be a freeing and liberating experience. To understand how this is possible, consider the opposite—being trapped and enslaved by oneself. This happens more than you think. Consider your own life at the present time. What makes you happy? What are the things that cause depression or anxiety? What are your greatest achievements and how did you accomplish them? What do you try to avoid at all cost?

Napoleon Hill (1937) in his *Think and Grow Rich* describes destiny in this way: "You are the master of your destiny. You can influence, direct, and control your own environment. You can make your life what you want it to be (p. 219)." On good days, this is a great and welcome imperative. You can conquer the world.

Brain research has revealed that the brain has a system for responding to positive stimuli and another system for responding to negative stimuli. The amygdala, an almond-shaped gray matter located in the limbic system of the brain, uses two-thirds of its neurons to detect negative experiences. Once the brain starts looking for the negative, the negative is quickly stored into long-term memory. For positive experiences to move from short- to long-term memory, they have to be experienced for more than twelve seconds. Rick Hanson (2010) describes the experience in this way: "The brain is like Velcro for negative experiences but like Teflon for positive ones."

To lead self in a positive manner, you need to develop a positive disposition toward life. Returning to those questions at the beginning of this section, consider more in depth what really makes you happy. How much of your time, energy, and resources do you put toward supporting that happiness?

What are the things that annoy you? How much of your time, energy, and resources do you put toward supporting that happiness? Chances are you spend more of your time, energy, and resources on things that do not even promote your happiness. Why is that?

Consider your working life. Do you really enjoy your job? Do you like what you do and the results you get from doing that job? Do you enjoy the people with whom you work? Why do you do this job?

Most people would respond that a job is necessary to provide all the other things you want in life—food, shelter, clothing, and entertainment. Employment is within our comfort zone—if you question that, try unemployment for six months or so. Most would agree that having a job is a necessity in life. But if your job or the people with whom you work are not promoting your happiness, why would you choose to spend time, energy, and resources on something that brings you down?

In chapter 5, we noted the importance of the 3 percent formula—part of the mathematics of leadership. Investing in yourself is needed for self-improvement and ultimately happiness. That 3 percent formula does not pertain to only the money and resources you allocate for self-improvement.

Consider using the 3 percent formula to pertain to each hour—approximately two minutes within the hour. Use the two minutes to exercise the brain in a positive way. One easy way to do this is to spend the two minutes in gratitude. For whom or for what are you grateful? Another positive thought builder could be what you anticipate for supper this evening or the walk you will be able to take after work. Gradually build positive thoughts. Remember, it takes twelve seconds to move a positive thought to long-term memory.

DISPOSITIONS OF REFLECTIVE INQUIRY AND SELF-TALK

Most leaders agree that reflective practice is a good and desirable mental model. During teacher preparation programs, candidates often reflect on their developing practice through written forms of reflection. This practice is well advised for the continued development of personal mastery.

Mastery may be considered superiority or control over someone or something. But it may also be considered attaining a level of proficiency. Senge (1990) describes it in this way: "Personal mastery is the discipline of continually clarifying and deepening our personal vision of focusing our energies, of developing patience, and seeing reality objectively . . . The discipline of self-mastery . . . starts with clarifying the things that really matter to us, living our lives in the service of our highest aspiration" (pp. 7–8).

Senge's discipline of personal mastery encompasses two components: clarifying what is important to the individual and learning how to see reality more clearly. Often, one can list those persons and things that are most important to the individual, but personal mastery requires clarifying what is important. Clarification takes additional reflection to free the mind of the ambiguity of why the person or object is important. The clarification leads to a second level for viewing reality.

To achieve this level of personal mastery, develop a reflective disposition. Most people hold inner (and sometimes outer) conversations. These monologues, this self-talk, provide the individual with opinions, evaluations, and remarks on what the self is doing while doing it. When the conversation is upbeat and realistic, this self-talk can boost productivity. The contrary is also true. If the self-talk is berating and harsh, the emotional impact can be devastating.

Linda Carbone (2014), a freelance book editor, describes on her website not only the benefits but the necessity of self-talk.

> When you talk to yourself, you're paying attention to someone who often gets short shrift in your life: you. If you berate yourself for behaving idiotically or painfully regret something you've done, obviously your self-talk is going to make you feel worse. But if you get a good dialogue going between you and yourself, you can make real headway in clarifying your thoughts and even lifting your mood. I'd go so far as to say the practice is a form of mindful self-compassion.

Carbone lists nine benefits to talking to yourself.

1. Give yourself a shout-out—compliment yourself on the way you handled a difficult situation, left your comfort zone for a new adventure, or just got through a busy day.
2. Give yourself a pep talk—self-talk can help you motivate *yourself* to achieve a goal at work, in a relationship, or in your personal behavior.
3. Debate both sides of a difficult position—saying your options out loud and elaborating on the pros and cons can help bring the right choice to light.
4. Blow off steam—if you're not the type to confront people who tick you off, talk to yourself about how they bother you or how unfair a situation is. Put the "self" back in self-assertion.
5. Understand your thoughts better—sometimes, we're sure we think one way, but our psyche tells us otherwise. Join a conversation with your subconscious.
6. Rehearse a difficult conversation—practice what you need to say (more about this in chapter 8, on using RISC).
7. Boost your memory—research indicates that saying where you are placing an object will help you remember.

8. Shake off stress and anxiety—work it through with a monologue.
9. Improve attention span and concentration—this helps bring a tangle of thoughts into focus.

Holding these self-conversations assists in clarifying personal vision and seeing reality more objectively. This disposition for reflective practice leads the self to an inner awareness that lays a foundation for considering others and leading with them to transform the organization.

WHAT IF THEY DON'T?

Jennifer says she believes all her students can learn. Jennifer says twelve students in her class of thirty-two can't help that they have learning issues. Jennifer says that this class is very far behind so they have to go more slowly. Jennifer says that she wants to teach them how to take notes but she knows they can't do this. Jenifer says that the special education teacher means well but there are too many challenges with these students.

Many people fall in love with suffering—especially if it is their own and whether the suffering is real or imagined. Jennifer's teacher mentor has made suggestions for each of these stated problems. For the note taking, her mentor provided her with ways to scaffold the notes with a fill-in-the-blank format. Jennifer had a reason why this would not work. Her special education teacher, who works in the classroom with her, suggested a way to rearrange the room so that the students with Individualized Education Programs could be strategically placed nearer Jennifer or the special education teacher. Jennifer had a reason why that would not work.

Clearly, Jennifer's self-talk is tuned to the negative stimuli of the brain system. The amygdala is working beyond the allocated two-third neuron portion to not only detect negativity but also create it. Jennifer has chosen to blame her students' lack of learning on outside forces that she identifies as beyond her. She justifies this reaction each time she produces a reason why she cannot address the needs of these students.

Ronald is notorious for his self-talk. By the time he arrives for work at school in the morning, he has had several conversations with himself, and in some cases, with others who cannot even hear him.

Ronald's self-talk begins with sleeping through his alarm clock and sounds like this: "You are so dumb. Why didn't you hear that alarm? I'll never make it on time." As he heads out the door, he remembers that his car is not parked in his usual spot because he got in late last night and his spot was taken. As he walks to his car in the rain (yes, he forgot his umbrella) his conversation continues: "These are the most inconsiderate people. They take a parking spot that belongs to someone else and think nothing of it." As he drives toward school, he calls out "Jerk!" to the person who just cut him off and "Learn to drive!" to the person who chooses not to make a right on red. By the time he enters his office, he is ready to take off the head of anyone he meets.

Thoughts are things. "When you say to yourself, 'I am going to have a pleasant visit or a pleasant journey,' you are literally sending elements and forces ahead of your body that will arrange things to make your visit or journey pleasant. . . . Our thoughts, or in other words, our state of mind, is ever at work 'fixing up' things good or bad in advance" (Mulford, 1908, p. 22).

In leading self, thoughts determine not only the outcome but all aspects of the journey. The courage to lead self begins with a single step toward the desired destination of where the self will arrive. Dispositions to lead self require the development of the mental post-it notes that develop the desired self and the qualities of mind and heart that influence our responses. As noted earlier, recognizing that power is not a four-letter word, that victimhood is optional, and that change is inevitable and growth is a choice forms the dispositions to lead self. Before the leader can lead anyone else, leading self is the constant disposition, the sine qua non of leading others.

REFERENCES

Allen, J. G., Wasicsko, M. M., & Chirichello, M. (2014). The missing link: Teaching the dispositions to lead. *International Journal of Educational Leadership Preparation*. Retrieved from http://files.eric.ed.gov/fulltext/EJ1024114.pdf

Carbone, L. (2014). 9 surprising benefits of talking to yourself. *Spirituality & Health*. Retrieved from http://spiritualityhealth.com/articles/9-surprising-benefits-talking-yourself

Dorfman, H. A. (2000). *The mental ABC's of pitching: A handbook for performance enhancement*. Lanham, MD: Roman & Littlefield.

Hanson, R. (2010). Confronting the negativity bias. *The Huffington Post*. Retrieved from http://www.huffingtonpost.com/rick-hanson-phd/be-mindful-not-intimidate_b_753646.html

Hill, N. (1937). *Think and grow rich*. Cleveland, OH: Ralston Society, 219.

Holter, A. C., & Frabutt, J. M. (2012). Mission driven and data informed leadership. *Catholic Education: A Journal of Inquiry and Practice* 15(2), 253–269. Open Access Journals at Boston College. Retrieved from http://ejournals.bc.edu/ojs/index.php/catholic/article/view/1935/1753

McGinnity, B. L., Seymour-Ford, J., & Andries, K. J. (2004). *Kindergarten*. Watertown, MA: Perkins History Museum, Perkins School for the Blind. Retrieved from www.perkins.org/history/people/anne-sullivan/valedictory-address

Mulford, P. (1908). *Thoughts are things: Essays collected from the White Cross Library*. London: G. Bell and Sons, 22.

Preidt, R. (2016, August 4). Blindness biggest fear for many Americans. *HealthDay News*. Retrieved from http://www.webmd.com/eye-health/news/20160804/blindness-biggest-fear-for-many-americans

Riccobono, M. A. (2016, July 5). The understanding of fear and the power of progress. Address at the Banquet of the Annual Convention of the National Federation of the Blind, Orlando, FL. Retrieved from https://nfb.org/images/nfb/publications/convent/banquet-speech-2016.html

Royal National Institute of Blind People. (2014). *Who was Helen Keller?* London, England: Author. Retrieved from https://help.rnib.org.uk/help/products-services/complex-needs-older/helen-keller#content

Senge, P. M. (1990). *The fifth discipline: The art & practice of the learning organization.* New York, NY: Doubleday Business.

REFLECTION—PART II: LEADING SELF

Vision/Mission
1. What is your vision?
2. Which stretch goals do you need to make to achieve your vision?
3. Which stretch goal is your first priority?
4. What steps are you willing to take to achieve this goal?
5. What will you commit to learning to achieve that goal?

Time Management
1. How do you use your 168 hours on a weekly basis?

Desire to Learn
1. Which dispositions describe you? What do others say about you (based on the disposition survey)?
2. How much congruence is there between your ratings of yourself and the ratings of others?
3. What in the results surprised you?
4. Which dispositions do you feel are strongly related to your leadership aspirations?

Self-Talk
1. What are the words, phrases, and statements you most often say to yourself or aloud? Where do these words lead you?
2. Realizing you become what you think, focus today on how you speak to yourself. What do you say when you are successful? What do you say when you do not meet your own expectations? What do you need to say more often and what will you eliminate from your self-talk?

Problem Solving
1. How do you view challenges?
2. What actions do you take to meet these challenges?

Part III

LEADING OTHERS TO LEAD THEMSELVES

Leadership is never a solitary endeavor. Real leadership is found when the leader can lead others to lead themselves.

This part looks at the many ways the leader works with colleagues to help them discover leadership from within. Sometimes referred to as *super-leadership*, this form of leadership is not about the hero, the superman, the born leader—but rather about how the leader taps into the potential of others and causes them to grow in leadership. While everyone has some level of self-leadership, leading others to lead themselves results in the spotlight on the followers in the role of leading.

Chapter 7

Find a Parade and Get in Front of It

"When we take people," thou wouldst say, "merely as they are, we make them worse; when we treat them as if they were what they should be, we improve them as far as they can be improved."

—Goethe

Goethe was telling us that if we treat people as they are, they will remain so, or, as he pessimistically puts it, they will become worse. On the other hand, if we treat them as they might be, they will become so. With what we now know about leading self, we can turn to leading others—to lead themselves!

Leading others is often conceived of as getting others to do as they are told. Other conceptions of leadership imply that it is possible to motivate others. The part that is omitted about leading others is that the goal is to help others to lead themselves. A self-evident principle of leadership is we can't make anyone do anything!

The knowledge required for leading others—to lead themselves—grows from the knowledge used to lead self. Leaders, and leaders to be, need to see the bigger picture, to know the motivation mismemes, to recognize that relationships are built one at a time, and how to use conflict—real conflict, conflict that is worthy of the name—to arrive at consensus and avoid the gunny sack of accumulated conflicts. This chapter examines the knowledge leaders need to lead others to lead themselves by seeing the bigger picture and using feedback, motivation, and conflict to treat others as if they are what they should be.

SEEING THE BIGGER PICTURE

Leaders know that "the measure of leadership is not the quality of the head, but the tone of the body. The signs of outstanding leadership appear primarily among the followers. Are the followers reaching their potential? Are they learning? Serving? Do they achieve the required results? Do they change with grace? Manage conflict?" (Depree, 1989, p. 10). Leaders know to use their offices the way a pilot uses a cockpit or an attendant uses the machinery in the ICU—to get the overview, the whole picture, so they can be immediately aware of anomalies that need attention. They know to build mental models to keep on track.

Leaders also know that small corrections made early can yield large results, similar to the corrections made by the *Apollo 13* crew when the command module failed. When that happened, *Apollo 13* was on a path that would cause it to miss Earth by 2,500 miles (Tate, 2015). To return home the astronauts had to fire the lunar module's big landing engine several times to get back on the right trajectory. Those who saw Ron Howard's movie, *Apollo 13* (Howard, 1995), saw the dramatization of how the astronauts stayed on target to get home to Earth by keeping Earth in the porthole so they could make small adjustments with bursts of the engine.

Who was the *Apollo 13* crew? Jack Swigert, thirty-eight at the time, was a first-time flyer. He was added to the crew just forty-eight hours prior to launch replacing Ken Mattingly, a prime crew member who became exposed to German measles. Jim Lovell, the commander of the mission, was the world's most traveled astronaut. He protested the removal of Mattingly. Rounding out the crew was Fred Haise, a backup crew member on *Apollo 8* and *Apollo 11*. This crew is famously remembered for the movie rendition with Lovell's utterance of "Houston, we have a problem."

When Earth moved out of sight—so to speak—of the small porthole, the astronauts made small corrections to get it back into view. These small corrections avoided a 2,500-mile miss and got them home to Earth instead of being lost in space! The leader who leads others to lead themselves knows not to let things fester; instead, the leader knows to make small corrections, while issues are small enough to be dealt with effectively and productively. Leaders also keep the bigger picture in view.

WHAT LEADERS KNOW ABOUT TEAMING

Apollo 13 was designated a "successful failure"—success in bringing the crew home safely, failure in the lunar landing (Lovell, 1975). *Apollo 13* was in flight for one week. The crew was named forty-eight hours prior to take off. The crisis unified the crew into a team!

If Lencioni (2016) is correct that being a team player is the most important quality that a person should develop to thrive in the world of work, then teaming should not be rare. In fact, team work should create leaders, not stifle them. According to Lencioni (2016), leaders who can "identify, hire, and cultivate . . . humble, hungry, smart employees" (p. x) have an advantage for their organizations. Leaders have to hire people who have competence, certainly, but also compassion; they must have the necessary knowledge but coupled with wisdom, and finally they have to do what they do with love, for their work, for those they work for, and those they work with.

A first question regarding teaming should be, Is a team really needed? Whenever a task needs to be accomplished, generally a team approach is considered. Teams should be formed only if individual skills are not sufficient to accomplish the designated task (Ling, 2012). Teams have the potential to exceed each individual's personal best. The resulting synergy is greater than all the individual work put together.

Teams and groups are not the same. Katzenbach and Smith (2006) make a distinction between the two. When people come together for a purpose, you have a group. You have a group at church services, you have a group at rock band performances, you have a group at the PTA meeting. Teams, often a subset of a group, come together to work interdependently toward a common goal. They have clear boundaries between members and nonmembers and generally have a low turnover rate, which allows them time and opportunity to learn how to work together. The *Apollo 13* crew had to work toward a common goal for mere survival. With limited time and opportunity to get to know each other, the focus was the common goal.

While some conceptions of leadership imply that it is possible to motivate others, leaders know that it is a self-evident principle of leadership that you can't make anyone do anything! That is why the goal of leading others is to lead those who lead themselves. The knowledge required for leading others to lead themselves grows from the knowledge used to lead self.

Critical to establishing a team is the leader's recognition of how each team member brings to the table his or her own mission and vision with established criteria in managing time and self-mastery. Individuals are welcomed to reflect and share these criteria as they continue to grow in leading themselves.

FEEDBACK AS THE LEARNING TOOL

Effective feedback is a critical skill leaders consistently demonstrate to engage others in realizing a common goal. Feedback informs individuals about progress toward the goal, obstacles on the way, and how individual contributions are making the goal possible. Just as important as giving feedback is the need for the leader to seek feedback and be open to its message. Five key leadership characteristics for giving and receiving feedback are trust, positivity, authenticity, accountability, and curiosity.

Leaders recognize that establishing a culture of trust sets the stage for performance. Before giving any feedback, that culture has to be well established. Conley (2017) describes giving feedback as a moment of trust. This opportunity will either build or weaken the trust relationship.

Giving feedback is not often a preferred task of leaders—especially if the feedback is less than positive. Prior to giving feedback, Conley suggests that the leader analyze the level of trust in the relationship between the giver and receiver of the feedback. Clarify the purpose for providing the feedback and the intended results from that feedback. Is this merely information? Is the receiver to make changes based on the feedback? Is the feedback meant to give a command? Is the feedback meant to invite new ideas? And finally, be sure the giver and receiver are clear about goals, roles, and expectations.

Conley (2017) presents five guidelines for giving feedback: (1) Give feedback on behaviors that can be changed, not on personality traits. (2) Be specific and descriptive in the feedback providing facts, not opinions or judgments. (3) Be timely with the feedback—provide feedback when the receiver can still use the information to make a difference. (4) Choose appropriate context for providing the feedback—a time and place where giver and receiver will be comfortable. (5) Make the feedback relevant by identifying what is positive, what area can be improved, and suggesting actions that can lead to authentic performance improvement.

Leaders know that how feedback is provided can cause an employee, a co-worker, or a colleague to leave a feedback session enthused to make changes that will bring about results. Feedback can also leave the receiver deflated, disgruntled, and diminished. Choose carefully how you will provide needed feedback.

MY BRAIN MADE ME DO IT

Leaders know what leadership is for, what to pay attention to; they know the motivation mismemes, and they know how to use conflict to arrive at consensus, a prelude to transformation. Although the idea that leaders can make subordinates do whatever they want them to do seems to help in general—we say it ourselves ("I had to do it," "how could I say 'no' "?—it is nonetheless a mismeme that ignores an unwritten and intuitive principle of leadership: you can't make anyone do anything! The corollary is that no one can make you do anything either.

Motivation cannot be external to a person. If motivation is the *will* to act (Duhigg, 2016), it seems intuitive that someone cannot be given *will*. However, it is true that consequences can be offered that may cause someone to make a decision or choose a different course of action. What might be an unpleasant responsibility might be accepted because of an underlying reason—to avoid unpleasant behavior, to keep a job, to protect one's reputation.

When leaders find themselves in a position where they have to *motivate* subordinates just to get them to do their jobs, John Maxwell (2016) has some advice. Leaders need to find out if organization members seem unmotivated because they lack ability or if it is attitude that renders them unproductive. Maxwell is adamant about employees' attitudes—remove the person whose attitudes are harmful to the team—even if employees have ability or are productive. If it is not a case of attitude, if the lack of motivation seems to have no evident cause, it is time to consider the physiology of the brain (Know Your Brain: Striatum, 2015).

The study of motivation has been part of the ongoing study of the brain. As neurologists map the functions of the parts of the brain, they recognize the role of the striatum in motivation. This small structure is located in the brain beneath the cortex, with its best-known function to be voluntary action, the *will* to act. A short section of behavioral and cognitive neuroscience highlights some research into the role of the striatum.

The past decade has seen dramatic change in understanding the role of the striatum in behavior. Recent advances from human neuroimaging research suggest a broader role in motivated learning. New findings indicate that the striatum represents multiple learning signals and also emphasize interactions between the striatum and other specialized brain systems for learning (Shohamy, 2011).

The article goes on to explain that the striatum is activated when there is anticipation of doing something pleasurable or of reward. As a result, the striatum is associated with movement toward and mediating rewarding experiences. Among other diverse aspects of cognition and behavior, the striatum's role in movement, reward, and motivation may be the most studied of its functions.

The operative word is *motivation*. It is not only the pleasure that motivates; it is also the *thought* of something pleasurable that might occur. When this function is impaired in some way, motivation may also be impaired. A leader knowledgeable about the functioning of the striatum may recognize other avenues available to engage a team member. Leaders know that habits are behaviors or thoughts that have become automated through repetition.

If team members seem uncooperative, perhaps some habits have formed that make them so. Habits may be triggered by a particular cue, situation, or event. Habits involve actions that are usually repeated over and over, are performed automatically with little conscious awareness, and are persistent and hard to break. Because habits are stored in the striatum, deep beneath the cortex, a malfunctioning striatum is seen when habits become disordered, such as obsessive-compulsive behaviors and addiction.

Perhaps uncooperative behavior has become a habit because of negative self-talk, that inner voice that repeats those subtle yet demeaning comments. If repeated, neurons in the prefrontal-striatal-midbrain circuit fire over and over, strengthening their connection and eventually (and simplistically) storing the thought as a habit (McKay, 2016). Self-talk has consequences!

So what is to be done? How can one grow in leadership to be able to deal with an unmotivated person, or worse, one who deliberately sabotages an organization or its leader, or a person who is difficult in other ways? Drs. Brinkman and Kirschner (2012) assure us that we are all somebody's difficult person, someone's problem! This situation requires the facet of problem solving to grow in leadership.

FROM CONFLICT TO PROBLEM SOLVING

What do leaders need to know about conflict? Brinkman and Kirschner's statement is based on research that the authors did in the 1980s to find out if attitude affected health. Their goal was to help others deal with difficult and emotional situations that can cause entropy in organizations, inertia and frustration in leaders. Their goal was to help build communication strength. To grow in leadership, leaders need to know about conflict so they can develop strategies for dealing with it.

Some consider conflict to be confrontation, dealing with difficult people or situations and negative or unwanted emotions. In fact, in this age of tweeting and texting, Sherry Turkle, in her book *Alone Together* (2012), found that even parents would rather tweet argumentative topics to their children rather than deal with the emotion arising from unpleasant topics!

Understandably, people want to avoid conflict at all costs. Fear of conflict appears inherent in programs designed to help people handle their emotions and negative feelings. Participants seek to deal with, resolve, mediate, avoid, and eliminate conflict. However, other definitions of conflict, such as disharmony, disunity, and incongruence, can be another way of looking at conflict. These definitions actually point to a transformational use for conflict when they are applied actively to enhance harmony, unity, and congruence (Kushner, 1996).

Looked at this way, what the leader grows to know is that conflict is to be encouraged, invited, and taken advantage of, not avoided, eliminated, or merely managed. To take advantage of the transformational uses of conflict requires two strongly held convictions.

One, a consensual, no-conflict approach to decision making is impossible. No single goal or process of attaining a single goal can exist in complex organizations and societies. Two, conflict serves important transformational purposes. It plays a part in organizing motives; broadening, strengthening, and clarifying values; detecting and correcting incongruence between organizational goals and individual behavior. The intended outcome is greater congruence between goals and action, belief and behavior, between what we say and what we do.

Mager (1997) humorously subtitled his *Analyzing Performance Problems* "*You Really Oughta Wanna*"! Performance problems may not be based solely on lack of motivation. Mager (1997) suggests asking several questions to determine reasons why "they're not doing what they should be doing" (p. 8). None mentions lack of motivation.

Is there actually a performance discrepancy?
Is it worth pursuing?
Is there a fast fix?
Are the consequences right side up?
Is performance punishing?
Is non performance rewarding?
Does it matter? (Are there any consequences at all?)
Are there other causes?
Is it a skill deficiency?
Could they ever do it?
Is the skill used often or seldom?
Can the task be simplified?
Are there other obstacles?
Can they do it? (Do they have what it takes?)

Notice that only one of the questions refers to the individual's abilities. Sounds reminiscent of Deming's theory (1982) that 85–97 percent of the problems come from the system not from the person! (More mathematical leadership!)

HOW TO WORK WITH A JERK

Dealing with a difficult situation is an event, while dealing with conflict is an ongoing process. Difficult situations, though they may have been *brewing* for a time, tend to erupt. Conflict lingers, remaining in the background like other important but not urgent things to do. Methods of dealing with difficult people or situations are often habitual, stimulus-response reactions. These methods may include choices to ignore, deny, argue, smooth over, acknowledge, accept, confront, talk through, manage, and avoid.

Methods of dealing with transformational conflict are assertive, seeking out opposing values to examine the lasting principles that undergird them. Disruptive, emotionally difficult situations and people often arise from the *gunny sack* approach to problem solving. Instead of the problems being dealt with as they occur, they are accumulated in a figurative *gunny sack* until it is heavy enough to use as a weapon. When the sack is finally filled to overflowing, the resulting emotion forces movement toward a solution, toward stopping the pain.

That is why the situation tends to be explosive no matter how long it has been brewing. Some individuals need the courage they get from anger to deal with a large problem because they lack the confidence and communication skills to handle small problems before they become so large as to be unbearable (Kushner, 1996).

MOVING BEYOND MANAGING CONFLICT

Within the bounds of safety and normal expectations of human behavior, choosing a response to a difficult situation makes it possible to move beyond conflict management to take further advantage of its transformational uses. Knowing how to use conflict transformationally requires sufficient time and conversation to permit emotion and strongly held feelings to be expressed. We need to "fight" long enough to figure out what we are fighting about. Because values are often accompanied by deeply held feelings, it is not uncommon for great emotion to be attached to the discussion.

The strategy for the leader is to be patient enough and permit enough conversation to take place so that eventually the feelings spend themselves. Group processes must occur in a setting where this can be done without recrimination and with sufficient time and acceptance of feelings. The leader must forgo the desire to finish the process, to get on with it, to get a decision made. It takes time to understand others' feelings about an issue. The hoped-for outcome is to be able to discuss the issue with full knowledge of the feelings attached to them.

Opposing values provide information about the underlying principles represented by what is valued. What this means is that the individuals involved can learn about the values held by both proponents and opponents of a decision or position. When these become evident, they can be examined for their congruence with organizational philosophy, mission, and goals. Used this way, conflict can help determine a course of action that incorporates the discovered values.

This is different from a vote where the majority prevails. When true conflict is present, it is essential that opposing values and feelings held on the matter be given time to be expressed. Strongly held opinions are often rooted in individuals' personal experiences. Discussing these feelings permits growth-producing interactions that use conflict transformationally to examine motives for decisions and helps leaders and members aim for higher motives and wiser decisions.

Used patiently, conflict can develop and strengthen relationships by permitting inquiry into underlying values that helps individuals learn from each other and the speaker can deal with the values at stake with less emotion. Used this way, conflict need not be feared because the emotions attached to beliefs and values are respected and used as information.

The organization and its subgroups become a small world, a laboratory of human relations, in which like-minded individuals of goodwill work very hard together to produce results that are important to them and engage in active, individual, and cooperative learning. Such interactions and learning connect behavior to goals in the supportive, respectful environment they create.

Developing the necessary frame of mind, learning, practicing the necessary skills, and striving for intended outcomes produce the advantages that can result from understanding and using conflict to arrive at consensus. The understanding, hearing what is said from the other person's point of view, is communication.

DIDN'T YOU HEAR WHAT I SAID?

Leaders know that communication is mostly a miracle that occurs when the message delivered is the message that is actually heard. Getting into the scarce space between people's ears is quite a challenge, not because there is nothing in that space, but because that space is taken up with so much of the listener's concerns.

The leader knows that the burden of communication is on the person with the message. If he or she did not hear it, it was not said: a tough bit of knowledge to accept. But it is knowledge that the leader has to grow into. Blaming the listener for not hearing the message is like blaming the victim of a crime. Even when the leader knows the communication cycle, blaming the listener for not hearing is hubris and self-aggrandizement. For example, giving feedback is conceived as a necessary leadership activity. However, the giver might think of it as feedback or constructive criticism while the receiver conceives of it as negative criticism.

Chapter 7
WHAT IF THEY DON'T?

Weak leaders and those without the experience, knowledge, and skill needed to lead others to lead themselves allow destructive subordinates to use emotional deceit as a weapon. Such leaders enable manipulative people to use emotion and to cover up their lack of substance. Conflict is the order of the day.

Drama queens/kings cannot stand to be confronted about wrongdoing and/or lack of performance, so they are quick to blame someone or something for these shortcomings. They are adept at habitually using emotional tirades that often include crocodile tears, blame shifting, a few lies, half-truths that they tell as naturally as breathing, and other trite and effective manipulations and histrionics to get away with their lack of substance and competence.

The leader who doesn't recognize and/or does nothing about these machinations is equally destructive to the organization and its competent members. Conflict—spoken or unspoken—is rampant. The legacy of these leaders is an ineffective organization, one in which mediocrity and protection of the status quo are the norm.

Real leaders don't play favorites, don't get involved in the drama, and certainly don't tolerate manipulative, self-serving behavior (Myatt, 2012). Real leaders who have grown into leadership by acquiring knowledge and practicing skill for leading self are best able to lead others to lead themselves.

Knowledge without wisdom can be dangerous. History has many examples: Stalin and Hitler, for example, and the knowledgeable, skillful doctors who connived with them to experiment on human beings. When leaders themselves have credentials galore but act as though others do not know, they cannot lead; they can only require compliance—even when what the leaders knows is incomplete or incorrect. Similarly, to be competent but without compassion is to be sterile, to do the work for its own sake, without thought for those leaders with whom or for whom they work. Finally, to lead without love, passion, or relationships is to do sterile work as well. It results in a lack of staying power, in abdication of duty when possible and convenient.

Max DePree (1989), in *Leadership Is an Art*, provides a list of what happens when leaders don't . . . Among the items are: superficiality, injustice, arrogance, betrayal of ideas, principles, quality, considering the work an interruption, confusing pleasure and approval of themselves with meaning. These then result in hollow leadership—when change is needed and nothing happens.

This is not an uncommon occurrence. Elected leaders find themselves in positions where they choose not to act because they fear offending some people. Promises are made on the campaign trail, but once in office the leader neglects the role to lead others to lead themselves by ignoring constituents, hiding from the real issues, and catering to the few who are the loudest or can offer the most.

DePree (1989) invites leaders to consider leadership as owing things to the organization. He notes that leadership is not about a great or famous leader but rather about a leader who appears among the followers leading them to reach their potential, achieve required results, and change with grace. "The measure of leadership is not the quality of the head, but the tone of the body" (DePree, 1989, p. 10).

REFERENCES

Brinkman, R., & Kirschner, R. (2012). *Dealing with people you can't stand: How to bring out the best in people at their worst*, 3rd ed. New York, NY: McGraw-Hill.

Burke, E. (1770). Thoughts on the cause of present discontents. Retrieved from http://www.unilibrary.com/ebooks

Conley, R. (2017, January 8). How to give feedback that builds trust in a relationship. Leading with Trust. Retrieved from https://leadingwithtrust.com/

Deming, W. E. (1982). *Quality, productivity, and competitive position*. Cambridge, MA: Massachusetts Institute of Technology.

Depree, M. (1989). *Leadership is an art*. New York: Bantam Doubleday Dell. Retrieved from http://www.leadershipnow.com/leadershop/0324-8excerpt.html

Duhigg, C. (2016). *Smarter, faster, better: The secrets of being productive in life and business*. New York: Penguin Random House.

Howard, R. (1995). *Apollo 13* [motion picture]. Imagine Entertainment, Universal Pictures, United States.

Katzenbach, J., & Smith, D. (2006). *The wisdom of teams: Creating the high performance organization*. New York: Collins Business.

Know Your Brain: Striatum. (2015, February 15). Neuroscientifically Challenged. Retrieved from http://www.neuroscientificallychallenged.com/blog/know-your-brain-striatum

Kushner, S. R. (1996, January). New ways of dealing with conflict. *NASSP* 80(576), 104–108.

Lencioni, P. (2016). *The ideal team player: How to recognize and cultivate the three essential virtues*. Hoboken, NJ: Jossey-Bass.

Ling, G. (2012). Why large teams write bad songs. Retrieved from http://www.challenge.gov.sg/2012/07/why-large-teams-write-bad-songs/

Lovell, James A. (1975). Houston, we've had a problem. In Edgar M. Cortright (Ed.), *Apollo expeditions to the moon*. NASA SP-350. Washington, DC: NASA. Retrieved from https://history.nasa.gov/SP-350/ch-13-1.html

Mager, R. (1997). *Analyzing performance problems: You really oughta wanna*, 3rd ed. Atlanta, BA: Center for Effective Performance.

Maxwell, J. C. (2016). *What successful people know about leadership*. New York: Center Street.

McKay, S. (2016). Neuro-science insight: How to break bad habits. The Chopra Center. Retrieved from http://www.chopra.com/ccl/neuroscience-insight-how-to-break-bad-habits

Myatt, M. (2012, February 22). Five keys to dealing with workplace conflict. Forbes/Leadership. Retrieved from http://www.forbes.com/sites/mikemyatt/2012/02/22/5-keys-to-dealing-with-workplace-conflict/#584a68b015a0

Rothman, J. (2016, February 29). Shut up and sit down: Why the leaderhip industry rules. *The New Yorker*. Retrieved from http://www.newyorker.com/magazine/2016/02/29/our-dangerous-leadership-obsession

Shohamy, D. (2011, June 12). Learning and motivation in the human striatum. *Current Opinion in Neurobiology* 21(3), 408–414. doi:10.1016/j.conb.2011.05.009

Tate, K. (2015, April 13). How Apollo 13's dangerous survival mission worked. Space.com. Retrieved from http://www.space.com/29078-how-apollo-13-moon-accident-worked-infographic.html

Turkle, S. (2012). *Alone together: Why we expect more from technology and less from each other*. New York, NY: Basic Books.

Whyte, W. (1956). *The organization man*. New York: Simon & Schuster.

Chapter 8

Fusing Power and People

The first responsibility of a leader is to define reality. The last is to say thank you. In between the two, the leader must become a servant and a debtor. That sums up the progress of an artful leader.

—Max DePree

Knowledge about leading others is wasted if a leader does not have the skill to put that knowledge into practice. This chapter will consider the skills a leader needs to have to lead others to lead themselves.

Communication heads the list of skills needed for leading others. In this chapter, readers will examine how to seek and find common ground to communicate with—not to—others. Skill is needed to develop self-talk to change one's mind and behavior to communicate and to get others to do the same.

Other skill sets for leading others include teaming. Leaders will consider how to delegate by design, rather than by dumping, how to work with teams to design and conduct productive meetings, and how to use data in ways that allow others to change their minds and behaviors. Leaders need skills to lead others to convert conflict to consensus and to deal constructively with the inevitability of criticism, move from conformity to norms to internalization of norms and from maintenance-producing interactions to growth-producing interactions. This chapter will provide insights for fusing power and people to lead others to lead themselves.

TALK, SELF-TALK, AND THE MIRACLE OF COMMUNICATION

Communication has been described as a miracle. When two minds can arrive on the same page—that is, hearing and understanding what is meant and not just what was said—a miracle has occurred.

Volumes have been written on the art of communication. Equally recorded are the volumes reporting disasters resulting from mis communication. Leading others to lead themselves begins with the skill of communicating.

In a quick review of book titles on communication, similar ideas surface even in just reading the cover: crucial conversations, how to talk to anyone, difficult conversations, skills with people, everyone communicates but few connect, how to speak, how to listen, getting to yes—and the list goes on. The leader recognizes that communication requires a *with* approach rather than a communicating *to* approach.

Studies on communication generally agree on at least one common element: listening. Joelle Jay (2012), president of Pillar Consulting, proposes that good communication is key to good management. Without good communication, leaders fail to gain commitment from colleagues, attain organizational goals, or establish communities of mission and vision.

In her own studies on communication, Jay lists five strategies for effective communication, with listening as the first and most important element of effective communication. Listening not only hears the words while waiting to put in the next word but absorbs the message to understand what is being said by the other person. The leader allows the speaker the opportunity to finish speaking before making the next comment. The leader repeats back to the speaker what the leader heard and repeats this process until the speaker agrees that what was said was actually what was heard.

There are times to listen and times to speak. In emotionally charged situations, the leader needs to listen. From a personal perspective, the speaker needs acknowledgment that the speaker is being heard. If a leader ignores the emotional response, a gap can widen between the leader and the speaker. From a professional standpoint, clear thinking can be eroded in emotionally charged situations. Allowing the speaker to vent can move the speaker back to the real situation at hand once the emotional response has dissipated.

Jay (2012) notes that two other situations require the leader to listen: in team situations and when colleagues are sharing ideas. In team situations, multiple personalities are generally at work. The leader has to have the ability to hear and process all those ideas without jeopardizing the team goal. When others share ideas, the leader listens so as to keep them sharing, invite creativity, and promote healthy relationships among the team. When leaders stop listening, colleagues stop talking.

Facilitating is the next element of effective communication. Jay notes that facilitation involves a continuous three-step cycle: (1) hear what is said, (2) interpret what is said to the topic at hand, and (3) say something that connects what was said to move the conversation forward.

Another element of effective communication involves questioning. Depending on the information needed, different questions are asked. If the leader needs to learn information, open, closed, or probing questions could be used. The parent trying to determine what the child ate could use these types of questions:

OPEN: What have you eaten since breakfast?
CLOSED: Did you eat any candy?
PROBING: While you were at Jovany's house, did his mother give you anything to eat or drink?

Questions can be used to build relationships: what do you find supportive in our team meetings? Rhetorical and leading questions can get people to reflect or commit to a course of action: what would I need to do to get you on board with this project? To defuse a heated situation with a colleague, funnel questions get them to go into greater detail about the situation: How many times did you ask your mentor for feedback? What was your mentor's response each time? Although these questions will not necessarily eliminate the emotional reaction, the questions may give a pause to the feelings and an opportunity for the speaker to feel validated and heard. In using questions, the leader needs to allow enough time for the speaker to think and respond.

Discretion is always an element in effective communication—and in many other areas of leadership. Discretion is described as the freedom to act or make judgments on one's own and is often the distinguishing mark between a leader and manager. Leaders know when to use discretion.

Discretion relates to confidentiality and influence. No matter what the position, leaders have influence. How the influence is used impacts the personal and professional response of others. Leaders adopt a policy of discretion and confidentiality with their colleagues, thus resulting in a trusting relationship. Under no circumstances does the leader listen to any information that begins with "Did you hear?" or "Don't share this with anyone." Leaders take the position that if you tell me I act on this information. Leaders who talk behind the backs of their colleagues, gossip, show favoritism of any kind, exaggerate the truth, or play two sides of a situation cause colleagues to doubt and break down the lines of communication.

One final element of communication is directing. The leader uses this element with caution. Directing tells people what to do. This is a form of communication, and some regard this as the way to get people to do what you want. Listening, facilitating, questioning, and discretion can generally accomplish the same desired result in a more collegial approach. Beware of directing to get what you think you may want. The end result may more often become an attitude of "I do just what they tell me to do around here" (Jay, 2012).

USING RISC

Leading others to lead themselves following effective communication directives can lead to wondering if leaders have to take what is given to them and keep quiet to remain effective. Knowing when to speak is as important as knowing when to remain silent. Knowing how to speak is just as important. How does the leader address those situations that need to be addressed? RISC is a four-step process for communicating a needed change.

The acronym *RISC* describes how to address a situation that needs immediate action for change. *R*—report the action; *I*—state the impact the action has; *S*—state the preferred action; *C*—state the consequences if the action does not change.

Laura knew she had to address the lateness issue with Sharon. She was a new mom returning to a former job. Returning to work may not have been her preferred option, but it was her choice. Laura, the tender-hearted boss, understood. She, too, was a mom. Yet, she still needed to address the issue. Sharon's colleagues needed her on-time presence.

Laura developed her RISC script as detailed in figure 8.1. Sharon was using a behavior that could not continue, and Laura focused her remarks on the behavior and not on Sharon.

Laura gave Sharon the opportunity to lead herself. Remaining focused on Sharon's behavior helped Laura separate emotion from performance.

R—report the behavior	*Sharon, you are arriving at work fifteen to twenty minutes late almost every day since returning from maternity leave.*
I—state the impact this action has	*Sam and Cassandra are supervising your unit and responding to your production team in addition to their own supervisory responsibilities until you arrive.*
S—state the preferred behavior	*Your unit as well as all the units need you to be present at the start of the day to respond to the needs of your team.*
C—state the consequences if the behavior does not change	*Sharon, if you are not able to begin the day on time, you will need to request a transfer to the second or third shift.*

Figure 8.1. RISC Script

Reflecting on the needs of the organization as well as on possibilities of development for Sharon, Laura used the RISC script to help herself address the situation and respond to Sharon's need to respond realistically and honestly to her own situation.

TEAMING TALENT

Leaders recognize they do not have all the answers and cannot accomplish all the tasks. Effective leaders surround themselves with effective colleagues and work with those colleagues to make them even more effective—that is, to lead them to lead themselves.

Teams come in all shapes and sizes: decision-making teams, consultative teams, coordinating teams, design teams, learning teams. As stated in chapter 7, teams work interdependently toward a common goal and have a low turnover rate, allowing them time and opportunity to know each other and work together. Effective leaders know how to form teams and work with those teams.

Just as with any group, a team experiences a developmental process. Based on Tuckman's model of the life cycle of groups, teams progress through forming, storming, norming, and performing stages (Boneright, 2010). Another model developed through Lencioni's work with teams focuses on relationships and norms in teams. Lencioni identifies five attributes in the model to achieve performance results:

(1) Members trust each other.

> Trust occurs when team members are able to be vulnerable to one another and are willing to admit their mistakes, acknowledge their weaknesses, or ask for help. Without a certain comfort level among team members, a foundation of trust is impossible.

(2) Engage in debate around ideas.

> Trust builds the foundation for teams to engage in unfiltered, passionate debate about key issues, alleviating two problems. First, encouraging healthy conflict actually decreases the likelihood of destructive, back-channel sniping. Second, it leads to optimal decision making because the team benefits from the true ideas and perspectives of its members.

(3) Commit to decisions and plans of action.

> Team members can truly commit to decisions because they are part of the decision-making process (done through a healthy exchange of ideas).

This often creates an environment of clarity and empowerment in an organization.

(4) Hold each other accountable.

When a team commits to a clear plan of action, peer-to-peer accountability can occur. An individual, for example, can privately point out to his or her teammate about their counterproductive actions and behaviors because the desired actions and behaviors were agreed upon in the first place.

(5) Focus on achievement of collected results.

When team members hold one another accountable, they increase the likelihood that collective team results will become more important than individual ego and recognition. When this occurs, performance improves and the team continues to thrive (Lencioni, 2002).

Having a team and having an effective team can be two different scenarios. In addition to working interdependently and with membership stability, Hackman, Wageman, and Fisher (2009) emphasize the direction this team takes. The overall purpose of the team is challenging and clear and engages the talents of each member. The task is meaningful, and members decide on work procedures. Members identify norms of conduct and specify what is acceptable and what is not. Systems are in place to provide positive consequences for exceptional team performance, educational opportunities to enhance learning of all team members, and required data and information for the team to carry out the project. Expert coaching is available to the team to make good use of resources. Effective teams learn how to work together and maintain healthy interpersonal relationships.

High-performing teams can be one of the most effective ways to lead others to lead themselves. They distinguish themselves by having a balance between inquiry and advocacy, have more positive than negative exchanges, and have equal attention on being inwardly and outwardly focused (Losada & Heaphy, 2004). To lead others to lead themselves, a safe environment for teaming has to be a part of the culture. Leaders make this possible by being accessible and approachable, inviting participantship, using failures for learning, and raising levels of expectations while holding people accountable.

LEADERSHIP GETS THINGS DONE

Getting things done means decisions have to be made. Decision making is at the heart of leadership. Deciding means choosing among possible courses of action;

decisions need to be data based, be informed, be participative, be democratic, be effective, be productive, be results based, and stick. Some decisions just move things around; others cause other action to happen. Decision making is leadership. No one person has all the information with which to make a decision.

When the district officials in South Avendale, Ohio, decided that data would improve the failing school system by informing principals and teachers of achievement, nothing happened because no one did anything (Duhigg, 2016). When a different decision was made about the same data, something else happened. Instead of having access to the data, faculty and staff were asked to make notes about the data that they copied to index cards. Next, they made a chart to match the notes and then wrote in words what they learned while taking notes and making the chart. After this decision, student results improved.

When the school district studied this phenomenon, they found that it was the interaction with the data that made the difference, not the data itself. Once the data was understood, it became information that could be used—knowledge. Once the knowledge was in place, decisions could be made using what was known. So, it is the data that drives the decision; it was a decision that turned data into information, the information into knowledge that served to help make wise decisions.

AGILE DECISION MAKING

Jim Highsmith (2011) is a prolific writer who blogs about leadership. He has some thoughts on agile decision making. Jim believes a good leader has vision, takes on the teaching role of leadership, and accepts the roles of decision maker, teacher, motivator, and facilitator, among others. But, first and foremost, the leader makes decisions! Highsmith asks his reader to think about a leader's decisions that are harmful to the organization: when does that happen? At what point does a leader's decision making damage self-organization?

Highsmith posits several checkpoints to look out for: the team loses respect for the leader; the decisions are unilateral, arbitrary, or even whimsical; there is no participation in the decision. Those unilateral decisions will probably be ignored. But what causes loss of respect? When the manager begins making unilateral or arbitrary decisions. The more unilateral the decisions, the less participation from the team, and the less likely the decisions are to be effectively implemented.

Every team and situation are different, so there isn't a quantitative answer to the question of how many unilateral decisions are too many. However, even though presenting absolute numbers risks misinterpretation, Highsmith believes the following guidelines may help define appropriate levels of leader decision making that will continue to foster self-organization.

Highsmith's rough guide is one unilateral decision every month or two and three to four decisions per month with team involvement. The hundreds of other decisions may be delegated to the team. In practice, few good managers make completely unilateral decisions—they normally talk issues over with at least key members of their team. But occasionally there is a need to get things moving by making a unilateral decision. In that same vein, it is appropriate for leaders to make certain decisions without team participation, but if they are making more than three or four of such decisions per month, according to Highsmith, even with team involvement, they are probably too absorbed in the details.

Another issue related to management decision making is the leader's job of absorbing ambiguity. In fast-moving product development efforts in which key decisions must be made quickly, consensus (unanimous) decision making fails. But even participatory decision making can get mired in discussion and debate. Many product development issues, both technical and administrative, may be fuzzy and ambiguous. In these cases, after participation has evolved to a certain point, managers have to be willing to make final decisions. "Well, the information available to us isn't crystal clear, but to move forward with the project, we'll go in this direction."

Leaders often have to bring clarity to ambiguous situations—and teams work better because of it. Self-organization does not mean abdication of leader decision making but careful evaluation of when and where each entity needs to make decisions. Good leaders have earned the credibility to make these decisions. The technical staff respect the leader's judgment (based on previous actions taken), participate in the analysis and debate process, and willingly accept the decision to move on.

The leader has absorbed the ambiguity of the situation, whereas leaving the decision to consensus would have bogged the project down in interminable debate. Good leaders know when to step in and take charge and when to encourage the team to take charge. They also know when to dig into why team decision making isn't working as it should. There is a lot of mis information, mis-definition, and misinterpretation of information about self-organization in the community of agile leadership. Good teams are empowered and experience a degree of autonomy—the best teams also understand there are limits in each of these areas (Highsmith, 2011).

THE TOYOTA WAY!

Charles Duhigg (2016) recounts the way Toyota's decisions brought an American car-making plant from moribund to productive by teaching American auto workers that employees have the right and duty to stop production when a car is not error free. The lesson was hard to learn because the time-is-money culture made taking time to make corrections a problem rather than a benefit. Workers were very conscious of the money frame of reference—every time the production line stopped, the cost was $15,000!

How did Toyota change this culture? By letting action speak louder than words.

TALK IS CHEAP

The Toyota manager who had the job of improving the productivity and quality of the cars worked the line and pulled the cord when an imperfect piece went through. This gave courage to others on the line to make quality the culture. The improvement journey resulted in obvious quality improvement that eventually meant not just money but also a priceless reputation. The manager knew that skill included caring whether the receiver actually got the message.

WHY DON'T THEY EVER? HOW COME THEY NEVER?

Leaders learn to recognize the triggers for a habit of bad behavior. By calling attention to the triggers, the leader has the skill to override the bad-habit trigger by changing the subject or relating a request to a prior success. The leader's skill is passed along to the team member and calls attention to the need to recognize the trigger, think about the desired behavior, action, or thought. Because unwanted behavior is the result of habitual behavior, forming a new habit that is enjoyable and rewarding will engage the dopaminergic neurons in the prefrontal cortex-striatal-midbrain circuit and make the process of wiring in the new habits quicker and easier. Aristotle once said, "We are what we repeatedly do. Excellence, then, is not an act, but a habit" (McKay, n.d.).

To lead others, the leader must be steeped in the knowledge, skills, and dispositions for leading self. With these elements firmly established and yet still developing in the life of the potential leader, the leader undertakes the development of the skills for leading others.

WHY DO PEOPLE DO THINGS?

Having the skill to lead others to lead themselves includes helping others get to the root causes of their behavior, realize that they are the actors and the authors of their behavior, to accept that change and conflict are inevitable, that growth is optional, and that taking on a victim role is a choice. An intuitive principle of leadership is that *you can't make anyone do anything!* People do things for a variety of reasons, for different reasons at different times. For leaders to act on the assumption that they know what someone is thinking and deciding why they are acting the way they do is folly.

In the *Art of the Leader*, Cohen (1990) reproduces a survey of factors that asks respondents to arrange work factors in order of importance to them. Managers and CEOs thought pay, benefits, and job security would lead the list. In fact, workers gave high scores and top ranking to working with people who treat them with respect, interesting work, recognition for good work, and a chance to develop skills. Job security, high pay, and good benefits were the bottom three (Cohen, 1990, pp. 140–141). Leaders and managers who make assumptions about what motivates people will take ineffective steps when leading others. Leading others to lead themselves means understanding motivation and providing a context where these elements can be part of the job.

Gene is an example of a motivated worker. He proudly associates with colleagues with whom he worked to design the prototype that was presented to the "higher ups," as he called them. He worked with a group of colleagues who were glad to work with him because they respected his ideas. There was challenge in the job, and he had the opportunity to do some design thinking. He was pleased and satisfied that he had the opportunity to think for himself without having to carry out someone else's instruction.

CONFLICT AS TRANSFORMATION

Whether caused by habit, personality, or disposition, difficulties with team members require the leader to act on knowing the difference between difficult people and situations or conflict. Leaders need the skill to use conflict—real conflict, conflict worthy of the name—to engage its transformative power.

Producing transformational results from conflict requires the confidence to deal with difficult situations, choose appropriate problem-solving behavior, manage one's own responses, and create options where there seem to be none. Many of the programs that deal with conflict management suggest ways to work with a jerk and to deal with a backstabber, a snake, a passive-aggressive person, a martyr. The desired solution is one that makes people feel vindicated or less victimized, one that helps them *win*. Choosing to deal transformationally with conflict requires a change of mind about what it means to win. Regardless of the outcome, winning means to

> *acknowledge* the problem without taking or placing blame. You do not have to accept the blame or responsibility for it; you merely have to let the person know you agree that his or her problem is a problem.

seek a common focus rather than dealing in accusations and recriminations; this is relatively easy in a school because both parties can focus on what is best for the youngster. You can, figuratively and literally, stand or sit side by side on a matter involving a student instead of being on opposite sides of the desk and the problem. In business organizations, this same approach can be effective if the focus remains on the vision.

keep open the lines of communication rather than give an ultimatum or banish the person or problem. Don't underestimate the power of the time out! It is better to defer a decision or judgment or ultimatum by admitting an impasse and asking for a postponement; this allows both parties to reconsider and come together again when they are at their best rather than at their emotional worst.

maintain professionalism no matter how you are treated. Your repertoire of strategies must include the ability to act and not react. If you have been able to speak calmly, with conviction and genuine concern, you will have maintained professionalism, which is to win in a difficult situation.

WHAT HAPPENS IF THEY DON'T?

When data is produced for its own sake and no action results from it, bookshelves are neatly arranged with clearly identified binders—the data becomes an office decoration. If data does not produce an action, the data might as well be carried around in a knapsack and displayed everywhere and then put back into the knapsack for safe keeping.

Cal's job as a data manager required him to provide data-based reports and a dashboard with evidence of activities. Before each quarterly board meeting, Cal found ways to enter the data so that the dashboard had information he could present to the board. No one in the organization saw the dashboard. He was the only one. Even hiring auxiliary staff for data training resulted in compliance but no real understanding of how the data was to be used for improvement within the organization. Lots of time and money went into gathering data but no improvement resulted.

Cal is a perfect example of what happens when leaders do not team. Leading others to lead themselves is not meant to lead to isolationism. Studies have found that when individuals mentally or attitudinally withdraw from the work environment, they not only have weaker productivity, motivation, and performance, their withdrawal impacts the other teams.

Cal's quarterly reports replete with data that only Cal contributed and reviewed enhanced the isolation of the organization as well as Cal's contribution to the culture of teaming. The numbers were static and so was the use of the data. Cal fulfilled the mandate to get things done and could adequately report "I just do what they tell me to do around here."

One wonders who even knows about Cal's existence. Cal remains at the level of conformity. Maintenance is operative but growth is flatlined. While this phenomenon clearly paints the picture of the disconnection of Cal from his data reports, his colleagues, and his self-worth to this organization, this scenario also gives insight to the need for growth-producing interactions for the organization. Leading others to lead themselves fuses power with people and results in internalizing growth-producing norms.

REFERENCES

Boneright, D. A. (2010). 40 years of storming: A historical review of Tuckman's model of small group development. *Human Resource Development International* 13, 111–120.

Cohen, W. (1990). *The art of the leader*. Englewood Cliffs, NJ: Prentice-Hall Trade.

Duhigg, C. (2016). *Smarter, faster, better: The secrets of being productive in life and business*. New York: Penguin Random House.

Hackman, J. R., Wageman, R., & Fisher, C. M. (2009). Leading teams when the time is right: Finding the best moments to act. *Organizational Dynamics* 38(3), 192–203.

Highsmith, J. (2011, August 2). Leadership and decision-making: Agile leadership. Retrieved from http://www.allaboutagile.com/leadership-and-decision-making/

Jay, J. K. (2012). Communicate well: Five strategies to enhance your managerial communication skills. Retrieved from http://careers.pda.org/2012/08/communicate-well-five-strategies-to-enhance-your-managerial-communication-skills/

Kushner, S. R. (1996, January). New ways of dealing with conflict. *NASSP* 80, 104–108.

Lencioni, P. (2002). *The five dysfunctions of a team: A leadership fable*. New York: Jossey-Bass.

Losada, M., & Heaphy, E. (2004). The role of positivity and connectivity in the performance of business teams. *American Behavioral Scientist* 47(6), 740–765.

McKay, S. (n.d.). Neuro-science insight: How to break bad habits. The Chopra Center. Retrieved from http://www.chopra.com/ccl/neuroscience-insight-how-to-break-bad-habits

Chapter 9

From Dependence to Independence to Interdependence

> *A hundred times every day I remind myself that my inner and outer life depend on the labors of other men, living and dead, and that I must exert myself in order to give in the same measure as I have received and am still receiving.*
>
> —Albert Einstein

This chapter considers the dispositions of mind and heart leaders need to cultivate to lead others and lead with others. Dissatisfaction with what is is the beginning of improvement. The leader must lead with the disposition that no one works as hard as he or she can to fail.

The leader realizes that no one can be forced to change but only invited to grow. If we treat people as they are, they will remain so; if we treat them as they might be, they will become so. Recognizing that power is not a four-letter word, leaders are disposed to plan, think, and do. They also recognize that self-interest on their own part or on the part of others is not necessarily selfish. External supervision may correct errors but only internal supervision can prevent them.

HABITS OF MIND AND HEART

Habits of mind represent dispositions that influence thinking and emotional responses, dispositions that leave mental and emotional room for critical thinking and creativity. Trust and honesty are dispositions that permit the kind of communication needed to deal with problems, difficult people, and difficult situations as well as to plan and celebrate the impact of good work. Effective mental habits are the result of executive functioning and emotional intelligence that help with self-regulation (leading self). Such dispositions enhance thinking and learning so that leading with others is possible.

Habits of heart contribute to the development and use of social-emotional intelligence. These habits are dispositions of care, honor, and respect for others' emotions and their worldview. These dispositions rely on the ability, capacity, and skill to perceive, assess, and manage one's own emotions when dealing with those of other individuals and groups (Coalition of Essential Schools, n.d.).

DISSATISFACTION: THE BEGINNING OF IMPROVEMENT

When dissatisfaction with what is is expressed, the leader needs the disposition to recognize a complaint as a possible area for improvement. Such a disposition looks for clues to improvement that come from complaints. Careful questioning and gathering of information from others lead to expressing the desired state and taking steps to make it happen. It may also lead to exchanging the language of complaint for the language of commitment, from "we can't stand this situation any longer!" to "we stand for something else!"

The leader disposed to lead others to lead themselves facilitates conviction and hope that the desired state might be accomplished. Holding the frame of mind that there are areas of improvement can be the impulse to find out more and encourage the language of transforming complaint into commitment. Leading others to think beyond the complaint into what might be and asking for a commitment to help make it so is leading others to lead themselves. Even though it might take place one person at a time, an incremental change can produce a large result (Kegan & Lahey, 2001).

Honesty is a needed disposition for leading others to lead themselves. Bennett (1993) in *The Book of Virtues* describes honesty this way:

> To be honest is to be real, genuine, authentic, and bona fide. To be dishonest is to be partly feigned, forged, fake, or fictitious. Honesty expresses both self-respect and respect for others. Dishonesty fully respects neither oneself nor others. Honesty imbues lives with openness, reliability, and candor; it expresses a disposition to live in the light. Dishonesty seeks shade, cover, or concealment. It is a disposition to live partly in the dark." (p. 599)

Leaders know that room for improvement is always present—if honesty is present also. How do companies like UPS stay at the top of their game? Although the company is not perfect (especially when you are waiting for that package!), Ron Wallace (2016) notes that 88 percent of the Fortune 500 companies on the 1955 list are now dead and buried. But not UPS. They are still on the list. What makes them different?

Jim Casey, the founder of UPS, noted it was always the little things that mattered. He practiced and inculcated constructive dissatisfaction in his company.

> I think we should test and check many of our present practices. Some of the things can be eliminated, and some can be improved. Among other things, I think we are using many useless reports. I think we are filling out forms that don't need to be filled out. I think we are doing a lot of work that accomplishes nothing, and we ought to study that and dispense with it as quickly as we can. (Wallace, 2016, p. 24)

No one, but especially leaders, should pretend that standards are being met when they are not.

Dissatisfaction does not mean this is no good. Leaders know about continual improvement. The leader welcomes the complaint, suggestion, and insight as the opportunity to move forward. Recognizing shortcomings and being constructively dissatisfied invites others to consider their own areas in need and starts the journey toward improvement.

THE PERCEPTION OF TRUST

Leaders do not freeze people where they are. Mischel conducted a famous study in the 1960s, on delayed gratification with four-year-olds who were given a marshmallow and told they could eat it immediately or if they waited until the researcher returned they would be given a second marshmallow. Research found some children ate the marshmallow immediately while others waited. Fourteen years later, those who waited were found to be more trustworthy, dependable, self-reliant, and confident than those who did not wait. What made the difference between those who waited and those who did not?

Trust pervades all parts of everyday experiences and is important in the healthy functioning of all relationships with others. It is an emotional act based on reliance. Oxytocin, a hormone and neurotransmitter in the brain, regulates levels of trust. The human brain is wired to trust others. In the absence of threat, oxytocin increases our trust level. For those raised in safe, nurturing, and caring environments, trust levels are greater. Studies have shown that trust levels can change based on life experiences. Trust is among the strongest predictors of a nation's wealth (Zak, 2008).

People do not automatically trust leaders these days. Life experiences alter the oxytocin levels in the brain. Trust needs to be earned. Trust needs to be cultivated. Leaders who lead others to lead themselves cultivate trust among the constituents. They monitor the use of *I* in their communications. They do not use *I* because they do not think *I*. They think *we* and *team* and they see their role as helping the team function. They take responsibility but give credit to the *we* (Drucker, 2006).

Leaders focused on cultures of trust are truth tellers in the organization. They tell what they are able to share and admit what they cannot reveal at all. They view promises made as unpaid debts. They talk about what really matters. They manage their own moods with consistent performance and predictability. They tell the same story to everyone not changing even minor details when the audience changes. They make people feel safe.

These leaders treat everyone with kindness and compassion, and they do good in their dealings with others. They find opportunities to encourage others and rejoice in their accomplishments. They strive to deliver great work with and for others (Martinuzzi, 2009).

Trust is a glue that holds an organization together. Like a house of cards, it takes time and patience to build and can be toppled with a single word.

PEOPLE ARE NOT WORKING AS HARD AS THEY CAN TO FAIL

No one wants to get less than an A. Everyone wants to be well thought of. Views of success can vary widely. The leader's perception of success may conflict with the performer's perception. Another conversation starter! The leader knows perception is all. How does the performer perceive her or his job or responsibility? Does the perception need to change? Does the responsibility need to be more clearly presented? The leader needs to determine whether retraining is required or a more serious corrective action needs to take place. In either course of action, the leader maintains a disposition of honor.

When Harriet's boss, Charles, told her that the presentation was fine but needed more visual support, she heard only the words that followed *but*! She crumpled under what she viewed as a criticism. She had worked for hours to meet the time and quality requirements to prepare and deliver the presentation. To hear a throwaway suggestion about more visuals meant to her that the job she did was unsatisfactory. If anyone had asked Charles what he meant by the feedback, he would have replied that he was someone who liked to see more than text. He really had no complaints about the presentation. What to do about this communication misfeed?

For one thing, if Charles was of the disposition that people in general, and Harriet in particular, weren't working as hard as they could to end up doing a bad job, then, with this disposition, he could have collaborated during some preparation time. That way, he could have encouraged a learning approach for Harriet to improve the design of the presentation. As an effective communicator who believed others needed to lead themselves, Charles could have created a context for Harriet to learn that it might have been more effective to include visuals in her presentation.

Charles's feedback—what he saw as a suggestion—required deconstructive criticism instead. Kegan and Lahey (2001) offer the language of deconstructive criticism to mean creating a context for learning rather than a means of fixing something. Furthermore, for Harriet to lead herself to an understanding that others' learning styles may be different from her presentation style, she needed to be the meaning maker and the one to make the choice.

For Charles, again, to simply ask, rather than tell, to be honest about his needs ("I have a tough time with text-intensive information. Can anything be done for me and others like me?"), might communicate to Harriet that she is in charge with an opportunity to improve her own communication to make sure her message is the one heard by the audience.

Charles and Harriet are just one example of dispositions in action. The dispositions that leaders need to lead with others can be cultivated. As presented earlier, all change begins with a change of mind. Recognizing this means that leading others to lead themselves requires habits of mind and heart that illustrate executive functioning—knowing that no one can be forced to change but only invited to grow.

POWER IS NOT A FOUR-LETTER WORD

When groups are asked whether they want power, answers vary from a resounding "yes" to a resounding "no" with variations between. Anecdotally, it seems that the response is gender related: Men have no problem saying they want power. Women, on the other hand, with few exceptions, want power to empower others but generally do not want power.

Personal power is not a four-letter word just because the experience or knowledge of power is coercive or abusive, demeaning or disrespectful, or even destructive. Folks think of people with power to be Hitler, Saddam Hussein, and other dictators and cruel persons who use power to meet their own ends. However, when asked whether Mother Teresa had power, the answer is usually "yes."

The moral of the exercise is to raise awareness that power, in and of itself, is not good or bad. Power simply gets things done. If the use of power is left to those with no conscience about how it is used, then the perceptions of power mentioned here will be justified.

However, those who are fearful of power and do not want power must remember that "it is sufficient for the triumph of evil that the good do nothing"! This quote is usually attributed to Edmund Burke (1770), perhaps an evolution of "when bad men combine, the good must associate; else they will fall, one by one, an unpitied sacrifice in a contemptible struggle" (p. 526). Those who want to get good things done must exercise personal power fueled by communication skill, belief in a purpose larger than oneself, and the never-ending effort to learn to use power to get good things done.

As noted earlier, if we treat people as they are, they will remain so; if we treat them as they might be, they will become so. Leaders who focus on maximizing the contributions of others as their right to guide their own destiny rather than bend to the will of another or to the whim of the leader promote self-leadership. These leaders focus on the "followers" and how to unleash their talents so they lead themselves as a part of their contribution to the organization. Self-goal setting and promoting positive self-expectation are but two ways to improve their performance (Manz & Sims, 2001).

The real power behind these leaders is in their own ability to model self-leadership. Former U.S. president Jimmy Carter still models his leadership at the age of ninety-two as he and his wife Roslyn respond to their passion of bridging the gap between the haves and the have-nots. The Carters have been involved with building homes with Habitat for Humanity for more than thirty years. The former national leader states, "It's a practical way to put my religious beliefs into practice over the years. We talk about poor people in need and this is the best way I know to close that gap between rich people and the people who've never had a decent place to live" (Dawson, 2016).

Those who lead others to lead themselves possess boundless optimism about the potential of others. They believe in the talents and possibilities of others—ordinary others—to accomplish extraordinary things. Of all the dispositions for leading others to lead themselves, this optimism makes the greatest strides.

LEADING FROM WITHIN

External supervision may correct errors but only internal supervision prevents them. To lead others to lead themselves requires the personal mastery to create productive thought patterns. These include the way others are perceived: seeking another's point of view, accepting ideas that are different from one's own, and believing that others are valuable, able, and worthy.

Parker Palmer (1998) in his advice to teachers states: "as important as methods may be, the most practical thing we can achieve in any kind of work is insight into what is happening inside us as we do it" (p. 5). While this advice may more strongly describe how to lead self, the message is as applicable for leading others to lead themselves.

Leading with others moves the organization toward a greater whole if this leading involves head and heart. Making logical, *smart*, and properly risky decisions require the head. Determining the personal and shared values of the decision requires the *heart*. Serving the shared values of stakeholders in the organization must always be the guiding compass.

Back in 2012, Google set out to find how to make the perfect team in a study known as Project Aristotle. In studying over 150 teams, some very similar in makeup and others very different and almost every shade in between, the researchers found that no pattern could be determined for why some teams worked and others did not. However, group norms were found to be a key to success.

Norms were described as the way the team members behaved with each other. Successful teams demonstrated two norms: team members spoke roughly the same amount of time, and team members were sensitive to how other members of the team felt based on tone of voice, expression, and other nonverbal cues. These human-centered qualities made the difference (Duhigg, 2016).

Leading from within requires a safety zone where team members see their work as important, as meaningful, and with clear goals and roles. Team members know they can count on each other and therefore feel safe to share what really matters—personally and organizationally. The dispositions to lead others to lead themselves in these organizations include a reality check at all levels to lead from within and without, to lead together to transform the organization. Part IV of this book explores this journey of transformation.

WHAT IF THEY DON'T?

Jack's story is illustrative. COO of a small organization, when Jack first arrived, his lack of defensiveness was refreshing. After several years of operating via a cult of personality, allowing new members to bypass their immediate supervisors and department heads to seek his approval that should have been given elsewhere, Jack became incensed because, "after all this time, they still don't trust me!"

Jack spoke regularly at semiannual meetings of the employees. On one occasion, Jack chose to speak to the group about communication. His message, in a nutshell, was as follows: "you better hear what I am saying!" After such an inauspicious start, totally lacking the disposition that the burden of communication is on the person with the message, Jack's defensive lack of understanding of his responsibility was disappointing to say the least.

Similarly, to be competent but without compassion is to be sterile, to do the work because it is there and to do it in the most expedient way possible, without thought for colleagues they work for or work with. Such a mode of operation results in a lack of staying power and in dereliction of duty. In the hubris of the ends justifying the means, the proper process is bypassed and the decision is capricious, whimsical, and made out of self-serving self-interest. Decisions are guided by "what's best for me in this situation" instead of by the mission and basic human principles of due process and respect for the individual.

If the mind and heart are not fully engaged, leading becomes commanding. The message cannot be heard through the constant proclamation of self. Interdependence reverts to dependence or worse—discouragement, disappointment, and defeat (Jack went full circle)—from dependence to independence to interdependence but reverted to the beginning. Jack forgot that his inner and outer life depended on the labors of others and that he had to exert himself to give in the measure he received.

REFERENCES

Bennett, W. J. (1993). *The book of virtues*. New York, NY: Simon & Schuster.

Burke, E. (1770). *Thoughts on the cause of the present discontents*. The Works of the Right Honourable Edmund Burke, Vol. 01.

Coalition of Essential Schools. (n.d.). Habits of mind and heart. Retrieved from http://essentialschools.org/benchmarks/habits-of-mind-and-heart/

Dawson, C. (2016, September 20). Former President Jimmy Carter's 32-year passion project to build homes. Retrieved from http://www.cnn.com/2016/09/20/us/iyw-carter-habit-for-humanity/

Drucker, P. J. (2006). *Managing the non-profit organization: Principles and practices*. New York: HarpersCollins Publishers.

Duhigg, C. (2016). *Smarter, faster, better: The secret of being productive in life and business*. New York, NY: Penguin Random House.

Kegan, R., & Lahey, L. L. (2001). The real reason people won't change. *Harvard Business Review*. Retrieved from http://ceewl.ca/12599-PDF-ENG.PDF#page=78

Manz, C. C., & Sims, H. P. (2001). *The new superleadership: Leading others to lead themselves*. Oakland, CA: Berrett-Koehler.

Martinuzzi, B. (2009). *The leader as a mensch: Become the kind of person others want to follow*. San Francisco, CA: Six Seconds Emotional Intelligence Press.

Palmer, P. (1998). *The courage to teach*. San Francisco, CA: Jossey-Bass.

Wallace, R. (2016). *Leadership lessons from a UPS driver: Delivering a culture of we, not me*. Oakland, CA: Berrett-Koehler.

Zak, P. J. (2008, June 1). The neurobiology of trust. *Scientific American*.

REFLECTION—PART III: LEADING OTHERS TO LEAD THEMSELVES

Vision/Mission

1. Do you ever talk about mission with your colleagues?
2. Are there activities outside work that you and your colleagues do together?

3. How is good news shared? How is bad news communicated?

Time Management
1. What kind of feedback have you received recently?
2. To whom have you given feedback recently? Why? What kind?
3. How often does your work require you to attend meetings? How long do the meetings last? Who decides how long meetings last?
4. Who gets things done in your organization? How?

Desire to Learn
1. Do you work with any teams in your job? How are your teams formed?
2. What was the most recent article, book, or magazine that two or more colleagues shared? Who suggested it?
3. What is the greatest asset of your team? What does the team need?

Self-Talk
1. Have you had any experiences that seemed bad at times but turned out all right in the end?
2. What successful failure had the greatest impact on colleagues?
3. Which conflict resulted in the greatest consensus?
4. To whom are you a difficult person?

Problem Solving
1. What steps do you take to address a touchy situation? What is considered tough?
2. Practice RISC to respond to a colleague who leaves the copier with a paper jam.

Part IV

LEADING/TRANSFORMING THE ORGANIZATION

A caterpillar transforms into a butterfly, a tadpole transforms into a frog, and a pile of bricks transforms into a wall. Transformer toys rearrange from one character to another. Tangrams transform from geometric shapes into boats, birds, and works of art. Origami transforms two-dimensional sheets of paper into three-dimensional works of art.

The point is that transformation does not require starting from scratch, getting all new parts or equipment. Transformation takes what is there and uses it to—well—transform itself. Organizational transformation in this work refers to becoming more so, more like the vision the organization has of itself. Transformation is probably not a radical change, but an evolving one. Dr. Covey reveals the transformation of annoyance into understanding in the story of the bus passenger surrounded by rowdy children. The children's father apologizes for them and tells the passenger that their mother just died. The mental disposition was transformed into one of empathy.

Organizational transformation means that individual dispositions are oriented toward the vision and group activity is guided by the vision. The organization becomes transformed into its vision on a continuing basis. The culture of the organization is transformed because the dispositions and behaviors and communication of the members have transformed from *me* to *we*, to vision centered and mission driven.

Chapter 10

All of Us Is Smarter than One of Us

> *Leadership over human beings is exercised when persons with certain motives and purposes mobilize, in competition or conflict with others, institutional, political, psychological, and other resources so as to arouse, engage, and satisfy the motives of followers . . . to realize goals mutually held by both leaders and followers.*
>
> —James MacGregor Burns

This chapter conceives of a misconception that leading an organization is based on the "superman" theory of leadership—that one person, the right person, can save or resurrect an organization. In truth, leading an organization is a matter of participantship, taking part, acting toward a goal, helping the organization become more of what it is intended to be. Leaders of organizations must have knowledge of how structure influences behavior, that compliance must evolve into commitment, and that growth-producing interactions must replace maintaining the status quo. Knowing how to use the ellipse as a metaphor for the organization relates individual goals to those of the organization.

TRANSFORMATION

Leadership expert James McGregor Burns introduced the concept of transformational leadership in his 1978 book *Leadership*, in which he defined leadership to be a process by which "leaders and their followers raise one another to higher levels of morality and motivation" (Burns, 1978, p. 20). Notice that transformation refers to higher levels, not changed, new, or different levels. That distinction is important to leading with others to transform the organization. The contention of this book is that growing in leadership is related to development in vision/mission, time, learning, problem solving, and reflection, through self-talk, the self-talk of Hammarskjöld (1965): "If only I may grow, firmer, simpler, quieter, warmer" (p. 93). With that in mind, organizational transformation to higher levels to reach its original purpose requires the same development.

Denis applied for a school start-up through the Design and Development Project. This project supports the development of new schools, redesigns drastically under-enrolled schools, or supports school flexibility and redesign. To complete the application, he relied on what he learned in a recent training program. The process was a rigorous four-phase review with cuts at the end of each round.

The first phase called for a narrative of the applicant's professional background, key elements of his school concept, and a history of demonstrated school leadership. During the first round of hearings, the application was sent back to the drawing board. Denis took it on the chin, added to the application, and, at the second round of hearings, was successful in getting the application approved for advancement to the second, third, and fourth phases. With a six-month start-up time to get a board and teachers for the new school, Denis began the search for just the right people to participate in this new endeavor.

LOOKING FOR LEADERS IN ALL THE WRONG PLACES

A misconception of leading an organization is based on the superman theory (Cherry, 2016) of leadership—that one person, the right person, a person born to lead—can lead, save, or resurrect an organization to make it profitable or effective. And, to paraphrase the song, organizational owners or boards "start lookin' for leaders in all the wrong places"! They look for those who have a past record even though that does not guarantee future success.

Instead, leading an organization is a matter of participantship, not waiting for "Mr. Right" (and it usually is *Mr*. Right). It means taking part, acting toward a goal, helping the organization reach its goal by helping it become more of what it is intended to be. Leaders of organizations need to know how structure influences behavior; how compliance, dependence, and wanting to please need to grow into commitment; and a process by which growth-producing interactions replace maintenance-producing interactions.

Guthrie (2013) posited that only by mastering complexity—both human and organizational—can leaders achieve alignment with vision, mission, and goals. Leaders also must be alert to their failings and graces to better serve the organization and to build the trust needed to reach vision, mission, goals. These characteristics apply to real-life leaders as well as to fictional heroes. His view points out the negative results of waiting for the superman, and worse, what happens when we get him! Barbara Tuchman (1984) pointed to the folly of ignoring one's own failings through self-aggrandizement—ignoring stakeholders' views and feedback and discounting their disaffection.

THE ANTIDOTE TO SUPERMAN

After the terrible tragedy of 9/11, more than one report of the event included the idea that a good thing about that terrible day was the way people helped each other. The only antidote to a cult of personality as leadership is a culture of participation. Individually, one can feel and be powerless against a superman. However, together, participants can produce a culture within a culture that provides opportunities for leadership at many levels.

Many can engage with simple as well as complex tasks. Each individual has a part to play that contributes to something larger—the organization, even the future. Knowing an individual's skills and talents helps the leader delegate by design rather than by dumping.

DELEGATION BY DESIGN

Delegation can be designed to develop a team member's confidence, to increase responsibility, to save time, to enhance and enlarge participantship. The levels of delegation range from "do as I say—this is the decision" to "take care of this" (Baker, 2014). In between are several layers of responsibility. When these layers are used to design an outcome, the leader can ask a team member to

- look into this; let me know the options I can choose from;
- look into this; let me know your recommendation so I can make the decision;
- explore this issue and make a decision; check with me before going ahead;
- work on this problem; here are the constraints; once you have something that deals with the constraints, go ahead with it; check with me if you have to (Baker, 2014).

Each level of delegation requires the leader's knowledge—of group dynamics, of the goals of the organization, of the skills and talents of the individual members. The leader needs skill at communicating and planning, and add to skill the simple belief that leaders can't be lone rangers, that participantship trumps followership, that everyone wants to be part of something larger. Honing their craft means leaders create leaders (Burns, 1978).

Given the imperative of participantship, the following question arises: which is more important, the individual or the organization? This question has a long genealogy. In the late 1950s, Whyte's (1956) *The Organization Man* dealt with the question of group think in which some described themselves as company men. It is true that our lives are defined and circumscribed by organizations. We are born into a family, go to school, go to work, join clubs, belong to churches and other organizations. In that belonging, how is individuality expressed? How are individual differences included in the life of the organization? How can issues that are felt deeply be dealt with? How is one individual supposed to be heard in the large organization? To whom does the organization belong to? Who is in charge? Who says what happens?

To ground the purpose of an organization in dignity and connectedness means that the individual cannot be disregarded when a conflict exists between the needs of the individual and the needs of the organization.

THINK WIN-WIN

Stephen Covey (1989) promoted effectiveness through the habit of thinking win-win. Dr. Covey elaborates on this concept of leading with others on his community website (Covey, n.d.). For him—and for the leader with the understanding that leading with others is needed to transform the organization—think win-win isn't about being nice, a quick-fix strategy, or a transactional one. Dr. Covey views it as character-based human interaction and collaboration.

That way, knowing and understanding the habit of win-win amounts to leading with others in a cooperative rather than a competitive stance. Win-win is a leader's frame of mind and heart that relies on mutual benefit to the individual and the organization. Dr. Covey describes the person or organization with a win-win attitude as possessing three characteristics:

1. Integrity: sticking with your true feelings, values, and commitments
2. Maturity: expressing your ideas and feelings with courage and consideration for the ideas and feelings of others
3. Abundance mentality: believing there is plenty for everyone

THE ELLIPSE AS A METAPHOR

Knowing about the mutuality of thinking win-win can add to understanding the importance of the individual and the organization. The issue is one of *and*, not *or*. Using the metaphor of the ellipse to illustrate this principle may be enlightening.

The circle can be an apt metaphor for mission. The center of the circle is its focal point, a center of attention. Every point on the circumference of the circle is the same distance from that center. Everything between the center and the circumference radiates from that center. The notion then is of singleness, of one thing necessary. Like a wheel, the center is the hub and the movement occurs because the center supports the spokes that support the rim and is moved forward by them. A circle can be drawn with a pencil and a piece of string (figure 10.1).

The point of a pencil is tied to the end of a string that is anchored at a point on a piece of paper or cardboard. The string is pulled taut and the pencil is

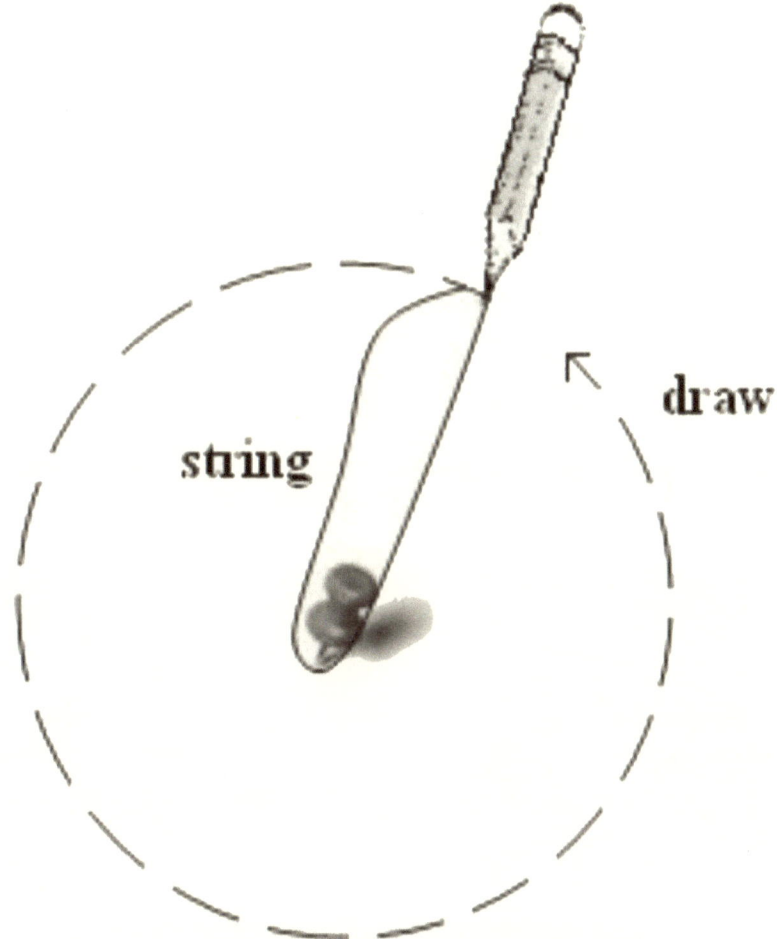

Figure 10.1.   Drawing a Circle. https://goo.gl/images/zw6oh6

rotated around the point. A circle is drawn as a result. The ellipse, on the other hand, has two focal points, and every point on the ellipse exists in relation to those two focal points.

To draw one the way a circle is drawn, the ends of a piece of string are attached to two places on a cardboard or paper. A pencil is placed inside the string and pulled taut (figure 10.2). When the pencil is rotated this time, the circle is flattened a bit, and the ellipse is drawn. Each point on the ellipse is the result of the length of the string (like it is for the circle). This time, each point on the ellipse is equal to the sum of the distances from the two points where the string is attached.

When applied to organizational life, one focal point of the ellipse can be said to represent the individual and the other focal point to represent the organization. Each individual has goals, purposes, and needs, as does the organization. The aims, goals, and needs of the individual are served by belonging to the organization. The goals, purposes, and needs of the organization are served by the individuals who belong to it. Individuals align themselves with the organization in the belief that personal or professional goals and needs are congruent with those of the organization. Belonging to and working for the goals of the organization helps individuals achieve their goals.

Every point on the ellipse represents a connection between the individual and the organization. There are places on the ellipse where the distance from

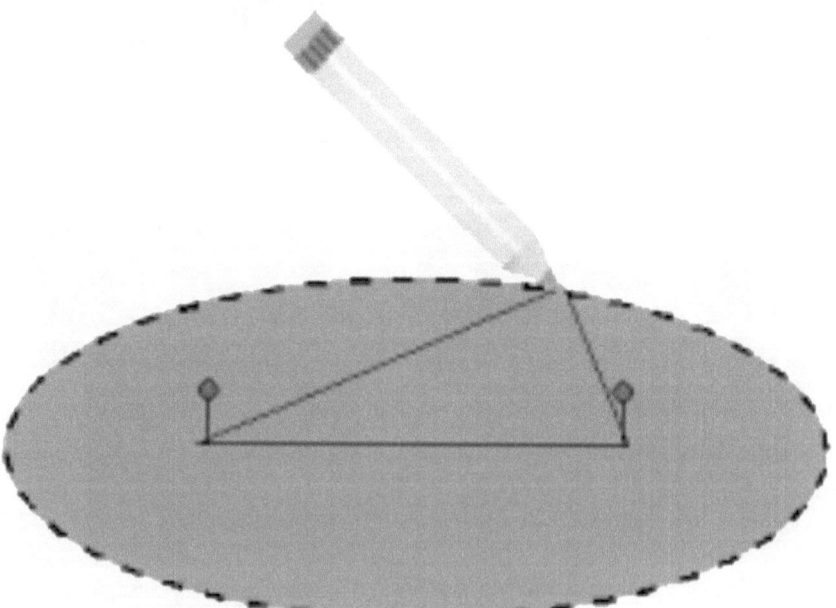

Figure 10.2.   Drawing an Ellipse. https://goo.gl/images/O8gM7r

the individual to the ellipse and that from the organization to the ellipse seem equal. This might represent the situation where individuals, working at a job they enjoy and are prepared for, can make a contribution from that position to the organization.

On the other hand, there are also points on the ellipse where it seems that the distance from the individual to the ellipse is greater than that from the organization to the ellipse. This might represent a situation like disability leave or retirement, where the individual seems not to be making a contribution to the organization but is receiving something from it. A point on the ellipse where the distance from the individual seems less than the distance from the organization might represent a situation where the needs of the organization take precedence over those of the individual in terms of needed resources and talent for staffing, funding, and so forth.

Individuals who associate themselves with an organization recognize the mutuality of achieving goals. A leader who knows the importance of relationships (Wheatley, 2006) also believes that it is possible to perform good works at work (Schreiner, n.d.) and that looking for perfection instead of progress is an exercise in frustration. Instead, the pursuit together is for excellence—not being number one, the only, the best. Instead, excellence is a continuing effort to surpass one's personal best (Pearson, 2000).

Knowing the importance of connectedness elevates the relation of the individual to the organization—to the members, to the past and present, and especially to the future. A leader with this knowledge believes information is to an organization what blood is to the body and does not withhold information out of self-aggrandizement or a "gotcha" or need/right to know. Finally, the knowledge of participation as an ethical imperative results in the belief and actions that the organization thrives on leading with others, others who are themselves able to lead self and with others to transform the organization into what it is intended to be.

Denis, with whom we began this chapter, did not look for participants in the new organization from among the list of "stars" touted publicly. Instead, he went to workplaces to watch potential members in action. When he saw mission in action, consistency in effort, belief in possibilities, he extended an invitation. The new school was founded on the belief that all of the children, regardless of their current achievement levels, would learn more through working with others than they could on their own.

Denis recognized the importance of the ellipse in developing the new school. His two focal points were learning and teaching. He understood his role in the process but recognized the necessity of teaming.

> As the school leader, I recognize that while I am the ultimate authority in making decisions that affect our school, teachers must also have the opportunity to lead each other as we work together to develop this new school. This includes

identifying the strengths of my teachers and leveraging a school community where each person feels personally attached to the school mission and plays an integral role in the school, outside of their classroom responsibilities. (Personal communication, August 21, 2012)

By having students and teachers work in groups and partnerships, they become comfortable articulating their knowledge, building off each other's ideas, appealing to their peers for help, and constructing cohesive representations of their long-term learning. The new school became the best in the district with the help of the teacher leaders Denis found. Leading with other leaders, he developed an organization dedicated to learning that surpassed its personal best every day.

STRUCTURE INFLUENCES BEHAVIOR

In his proposal for this new school, Denis envisioned the structure that needed to be in place. Organizational structure is how people are grouped together to accomplish a task or goal. The structure dictates the relationship between leaders and followers. Grouping people together in certain ways either promotes or prohibits effective behaviors. Leaders consider this in choosing a structure that will most effectively produce the culture for accomplishing the strategic goals of the organization.

A functional structure is a top-down hierarchy where decision making is made at the highest practical level. People work according to function—secretaries work together on secretarial tasks—and employees have narrowly focused jobs. Enforced rules predict the order. While employees may become proficient at their narrowly defined jobs, minimal opportunities for creativity exist. This model is used in the military to produce very predictable behaviors.

A team structure allows for a freer workplace environment. Teams are fluid, and they take charge of the goals, projects, and tasks of the organization. Authority is closer to the teams than management. Creativity, enthusiasm, and initiative are often more developed. Satisfaction increases as jobs become less specialized. However, this also can result in less efficiency.

At times, a divisional structure is needed. Employees are divided into a group that focuses on one area of concern. This structure often has decentralized power, yet increased control over the focused area. Oftentimes, managers learn to behave like leaders in this divisional structure.

Sometimes, an organization combines functional and divisional structures into a matrix, with the functional structure as permanent and individuals pulled from different areas to work on a divisional project. This structure can retain functional efficiency but often includes conflicts among the managers of the group leaving the employees caught between two bosses. Uncooperative behaviors can result and department conflicts surface.

The team structure inevitably has the greatest possibilities for moving from status quo to growth-producing interactions as long as team members rise to the challenge. Teams must be trained to flourish in their own expertise as well as in communication, diversity, and problem solving (Johnson, 2017).

FROM COMPLIANCE TO COMMITMENT

Most organizations have some level of safety compliance in place. This is often for the benefit of the organization as well as those impacted by the organization (the ellipse effect). When the organization works merely from a compliance standpoint, resentment, fear, and abdication of responsibility result. The difference is between what is required and what is possible and how the organization responds to making the difference.

Ask any two employees what is *effective*? While the word has a definition, the meaning can be quite different to each person. Compliant responses include numbers, regulations, and corporate descriptions with measures—laying bricks. Committed responses recognize the role of effectiveness for and by each individual—building a cathedral. What is required to be effective is different from what is possible.

Reporting effectiveness or ineffectiveness does not always lead to commitment. The assumption that everything is fine because no one is reporting otherwise is a false assumption. Often, informal methods for addressing any issue can provide the most valuable feedback through one-on-one interactions between leaders and followers.

Creating a culture of commitment necessitates building a culture of justice. Organizations that have great success understand that failures are generally not the fault of individuals but the faults of systems. Sidney Dekker (2001) says that human error is a symptom of trouble deeper in the system. True justice involves finding the system faults and fixing them rather than blaming individuals. In cultures of justice, employees do not feel that the organization is out to get them but rather cares about their well-being. This caring is contagious and thus further builds a culture of commitment.

WHAT IF THEY DON'T?

A new VP was hired. He, a tall, slim, garrulous sort, subscribed to the before-me-nothing-has-been-done proposition of leadership. It did not take long for employees to realize that they had better get on his good side to get any consideration. Frenetic, hyper, proud to have 2,000 emails a day—that he viewed while at meetings with other human beings—he turned over complainers and criticizers to chairpersons, positions that he created as he needed them to eliminate his responsibility for dealing with others' concerns.

His appointments were those whose flattery he believed, with or without qualification or competence for the job. As a result, he was surrounded by flatterers, never to hear the perceptions of those who disagreed (Tuchman, 1984). The result was a change in culture of the organization within three years to one of competing for his attention rather than one of cooperation with colleagues, who now became impediments to accomplishment if any one of them invoked his ire.

When a company reneged on a contractual agreement, this superman VP told the affected employee that she was on her own. Unable to engage the commitment of others was the kryptonite that paralyzed this superman. He simply abdicated his responsibility. The result was an organization of lone rangers, set upon self-interest that minimized the need to work for the common good. They worked instead for the superman's attention and approval.

Abuse of power and position followed easily, and the folly of self-aggrandizement infected the position. A cult of personality dominated the organization. Policies were ignored when inconvenient and invoked when needed, and decisions were made with no regard for individual dignity. Unilateral decision making—a form of bullying—became the norm. This structure influenced the behavior of all reverting to a status quo operation. Someone tangential to the organization remarked, "They don't like it if you speak your mind around here."

Fundamental to transforming the organization is the realization that the organization must constantly become more of what it is intended to be. The mission, vision, the hopes for the organization form the road map, as T. S. Eliot said "to arrive where we started." The superman VP believed he was the reason the organization existed. What his x-ray vision could not see was the lack of followers.

Leading with others to transform the organization requires a leader who recognizes his or her role. He or she has to turn separate initiatives into a program of change that is balanced and integrated. Attempting to change behaviors and capabilities of the followers will not transform but rather deform the organization. Teams are key building blocks, and the leader has to be seen as a member of the team. All of us—working together—is smarter than any one of us working alone. The next chapter examines the skills needed to transform the organization.

REFERENCES

Baker, T. (2014, August 2). The leader's journey: Understanding the 6 levels of delegation. Retrieved from https://www.linkedin.com/pulse/20140802174559-51769872-the-leader-s-journey-understanding-the-6-levels-of-delegation?trk=pulse-det-nav_art

Burns, J. M. (1978). *Leadership*. New York: Harper and Row.

Cherry, K. (2016, August 30). The major leadership theories: The eight major theories of leadership. Verywell.com. Retrieved from https://www.verywell.com/the-great-man-theory-of-leadership-2795311

Covey, S. R. (1989). *The 7 habits of highly effective people*. New York: Simon & Schuster.

Covey, S. R. (n.d.). *The 7 habits of highly effective people: Habit 4 think win-win*. Retrieved from from https://www.stephencovey.com/7habits/7habits-habit4.php

Dekker, S. (2001). The field guide to human error. Beddford, UK: Cranfiled University Press. Retrieved from http://www.leonardo-in-flight.nl/PDF/FieldGuide%20to%20Human%20Error.PDF

Guthrie, D. (2013, June 14). Looking for leaders, settling for superheroes. Retrieved from http://www.forbes.com/sites/dougguthrie/2013/06/14/looking-for-leaders-settling-for-superheroes/#6964dd481bc6

Hammarskjöld, D. (1965). *Markings*. New York, NY: Alfred A. Knopf.

Johnson, S. (2017). The effects of organizational structure on behavior. Retrieved from http://smallbusiness.chron.com/effects-organizational-structure-behavior-65759.html

Pearson, S. (2000). Personal best. Tools for Citizenship and Life. Retrieved from http://www.hope.edu/academic/education/wessman/2block/brainkeys/personalbest.htm

Schreiner, E. (n.d.). Five characteristics of a good work ethic. Retrieved from http://smallbusiness.chron.com/five-characteristics-good-work-ethic-10382.html

Tuchman, B. W. (1984). *The march of folly: From Troy to Vietnam*. New York: Random House.

Wheatley, M. (2006). *Leadership and the new science; Discovering order in a chaotic world*, 3rd ed. San Francisco, CA: Berret-Koehler.

Whyte, W. (1956). *The organization man*. New York: Simon & Schuster.

Chapter 11

If You Want to Be Smart, Hire Up

There is nothing more difficult to take in hand, more perilous to conduct, or more uncertain in its success, than to take the lead in the introduction of a new order of things.

—Niccolo Machiavelli

Leading with others to transform the organization requires the skill to engage stakeholders, to seek and find common ground, to recognize, and to choose small incremental change early enough to produce substantial results from beginning with the end in mind, the skill to synergize results in participantship—moving from dependence through independence into interdependence. This chapter examines skills leaders need to promote the transformation of the organization.

FROM NOT SO GOOD TO GREAT

Pat accepted the position of principal in an urban school. The former principal of thirty years was retiring. The superintendent invited Pat to become the principal. He met Pat at the school to provide a personal tour and to meet briefly with the outgoing principal.

First reactions should have been Pat's hint that there was more to this situation than met the eye. There were as many students in the hallway as in the classrooms. The noise level was intense—so much so that the secretary hardly heard the doorbell to alert her to the guests waiting outside. Disorder seemed to be the order of the day as books and papers were piled on windowsills, on the floor, in open cupboards, on every flat surface in each classroom visited.

The dress code seemed suspended for the day as shirttails were exposed, shoes were unlaced, and excessive jewelry and makeup were the fad.

Garbage filled every wastepaper basket and flowed onto the floor. The play yard and the grounds surrounding the school were littered with empty soda bottles, food wrappings, apple cores, and banana peels. Pathways between buildings were covered with grass cuttings and overgrown with weeds. The superintendent's comment "You know how the end of the year is" did not totally dissuade Pat from backing out of this contract.

Early July found Pat in the principal's seat. Students were gone, teachers were finished with end-of-the-school-year tasks, and the latest development was that the secretary also decided to take retirement. Pat pushed forward.

While viewing the building as an insider, Pat noted that at least the wastepaper cans had been emptied and many of the books were piled inside classroom closets. The amount of cleaning that needed to be accomplished seemed insurmountable even though there were two months to accomplish the task. The hallways remained so cluttered that even one person had difficulty passing through. Yet, with all this obvious need for order, Pat turned his attention to what he considered the reason the school existed—the students and their teachers.

For two weeks, Pat reviewed student and teacher records. He was pleasantly surprised to find students with high achievement, scoring As and Bs on most report cards. What he found puzzling was the lack of any standardized test scores, but he assumed they would eventually be located. In reviewing teacher records, he noted about a 50 percent retention rate, which seemed low compared to other schools where he had been employed. Faculty evaluations rated teachers as proficient or distinguished. He related this to why these students were such high performers.

The summer passed and the extensive hours of cleaning, reorganizing, planning, and meeting faculty and families resulted in starting the school year on time. The first days revealed what had become the norm in the school: arrival seemed to be anytime between 7:00 and 9:30—and this included the arrival time of teachers. Within the first few days, the chaos Pat had observed as a visitor back in the spring began to reveal its ugly head. Despite a dress code and school procedures, most of what would contribute to order was ignored. Parents felt it was their right to visit the classrooms of their children at any time, and teachers were to be available to them whenever they wanted. Changing this culture was the newest challenge but not the greatest one.

An area meeting of principals was held during the second week of the school year. This was when Pat first heard about the standardized test scores. Of the twenty-three schools in the region, schools were ranked in performance order, but no name was attached to the school—only a code. The focus for the meeting was the district's intent to improve math scores.

Various reports were made on performances of each school, including areas of mathematics that needed the greatest improvement, grade levels that seemed in most need of improvement, and the dollar amounts allocated for teacher development. After the reports were made, standardized test score results were distributed to each principal. As Pat reviewed the reports for this school, he realized that in every category, his school—Code 0723—ranked dead last. Pat was pretty certain that he had been duped.

Several thoughts pervaded Pat's thinking. If these test scores were so low, how were students getting As and Bs on their report cards? What kind of professional development had teachers received for math instruction and how was this implemented? What were parents told about their children's progress in mathematics? Most of these questions could be answered only through conversations with teachers.

That same day, Pat made an in-depth study of the math results. He examined which areas indicated the greatest need and if there were any classes that scored significantly (more than two years) below grade level. He wanted to have the data clear in his own mind before speaking with teachers.

Pat arranged to meet with all the teachers who taught math and invited all teachers to join in the meeting. To his surprise and theirs, they had no idea that their students had the lowest performance in the district. They had never seen standardized test results, although they knew students took these tests yearly.

When Pat asked how students were able to maintain at least a B average in math, teachers explained they were not allowed to give anything lower than a B in the major subjects. The former principal had made this edict and this kept parents happy—even if they were uninformed. Pat requested that teachers consider what they could do individually and what they could do collectively as a school to enhance student learning.

Within the week, Pat rearranged schedules to give priority time to math instruction. All grade levels now had an hour of math instruction each day. Pat requested that each grade level—PK-2, 3–5, and 6–8—select a grade-level leader who would represent the teachers and students of that level in deciding on and implementing the incremental changes needed. The grade-level teachers did their own study of the standardized test scores and noted that problem solving was an area that challenged all students. They also agreed that teaching problem solving challenged them. They needed help in this area.

Pat and the grade-level teachers constructed a plan for teacher improvement. A professional development plan was implemented, which included a once-a-week session during the scheduled planning sessions on teaching math problem solving and a biweekly visit by the grade-level leader to observe how the professional development was being implemented. Change was noted immediately—but not the kind of change Pat anticipated.

The first-grade teacher became "ill" and needed to take a leave of absence. Her doctor's note indicated that symptoms of stress may have been causing the illness. (Of course, she was one of the teachers who often came late to school and had already received two warnings with the next incident resulting in a write-up for her file. And this was just the first month of school.)

The fifth-grade teacher claimed she could not attend the professional development program because she had another job after school and the former principal allowed her to use the planning time to correct papers. When this same exemption was not granted by Pat, she too claimed mental distress as her issue. When she could not find a doctor to confer this "diagnosis," she resigned her position.

The seventh-grade math teacher claimed that her daughter who was a student in the school did not like the new changes and so she and her daughter were transferring schools. This happened by the end of the week. Within the first month of the school year, three math teachers were no longer a part of the staff. Substitutes were temporarily put in place as Pat spent endless hours interviewing teachers for the positions.

Meanwhile, the grade-level leaders continued with the weekly professional development meetings and began visiting math classes. With the sudden departure of the three teachers, a different culture started to emerge. Teachers began to talk with each other about the changes they were making in their teaching, more teachers made requests to visit each other's math classes, and teachers offered to cover classes to allow this observation to happen.

Pat spent more than four months interviewing teachers, observing demonstration lessons, and checking teacher references as well as assuming the teaching of some of the classes. This unsettled atmosphere in classrooms did not help to develop students' math skills, nor did it appease angry parents. Pat recognized that he had to make right choices in the hiring of these teachers if he wanted to make a difference for these students. By the end of January, Pat finally had a full staff once again but also had only five months left in the school year. Meanwhile, a group of teachers emerged to transform the school from not so good to moving toward greatness.

BEGINNING WITH THE END IN MIND

As Pat was forced to address the issues of hiring new teachers, this difficulty gave him the opportunity to change a culture of practice. Pat assumed the position of principal in this urban school because he believed all students could learn. The added challenge of being at the bottom of the math totem pole in the district only added to this opportunity. He recognized that the school could only get better because you cannot fall off the floor.

School culture has been defined in many ways but basically it is "the way things are done around here." Grange (2013) describes culture this way: "Culture is a complex, multi-faceted and multi-layered phenomenon that is socially learned and transmitted between people. It is about behaviors, beliefs, symbols, norms and expectations. It grows over time and can be directed and shaped with strong leadership and sound methodologies" (p. 3). Kotter (2012) affirms that culture changes only after people's actions and experiences have altered.

The culture of the school had been one of keeping people happy. Students were happy with their As and Bs. Parent were happy because their children were happy. Conflict was nearly nonexistent but so was learning. The reality of performing at the lowest level called for change.

Challenging mindsets is where true change happens. Pat gradually uncovered a culture of expediency that consequently robbed students of real-life learning and caused teachers to isolate themselves from the very people who most needed them. After the shock of being the lowest-performing school, Pat and his staff had two choices: to remain in this culture of cover-up or to take steps to transform the organization. Fortunately, Pat and several teachers chose the latter.

Pat and the teachers had first to envision multiple futures for the school and then force themselves to figure out which future had the potential to move them in a preferred direction. Although they may not have put a label on the process, Pat and these teachers undertook a restorative process that required a shift in hearts and minds. A restorative process is based on restorative justice, an alternative to punitive responses to wrongdoing. "Inspired by indigenous traditions, it brings together persons harmed with persons responsible for harm in a safe and respectful space, promoting dialogue, accountability, and a stronger sense of community" (Davis, 2014).

While no teacher or Pat himself would describe what they were doing as restoring justice to these students by implementing restorative practices, that in fact is what they set out to do. Thorsborne and Blood (2013) describe what a restorative school looks, feels, and sounds like:

- The school regards itself as a learning organization, committed to continual improvement.
- There is a comfortable marriage between the values of the school and the values of a restorative approach to problem-solving.
- Leadership is values-based and transformational, and leaders walk the talk, and model the required change.
- There is an understanding of the need to restore relationships in the aftermath of conflict and wrongdoing or major incidents within the school. This is reflected in practice [and] the focus of problem-solving is around the

damage that needs to be fixed rather the rule breach that needs to be punished and is solution-focused.
- There is clear and effective dialogue from the top down, bottom up and between staff, students, parents and anyone engaged with the school community.
- Professional development for adults takes a high priority and is resourced to reflect this.
- Language used is solution-focused and avoids blame.
- Everyone's voice is important, not just the voice of adults within the school community. There is more *listening* and less *telling*. (pp. 60–65)

There were no quick fixes to this situation. Shifting thinking and behaviors of the whole school community would take the next two years to realize the needed change.

HIRE UP

One decision-making step Pat implemented related to his hiring practice. As Pat interviewed potential teachers, he realized these newcomers would have an outsider's perspective. As is often the case for the new principal, Pat inherited teachers. These teachers worked with or for the previous principal, and they were acculturated in a climate that needed change. Initiating change is harder than introducing new ideas. New teachers did not have a past experience here, and thus they would come with a fresh perspective.

Another step Pat took in the hiring practice was seeking those who knew more about teaching and learning mathematics than he did. He recognized the hiring process as another opportunity to invite colleagues to assist with transforming this organization by getting the right people into the school. Pat invited (did not look for volunteers) two teachers to assist with the résumé review and interviews. This small team determined the current talent pool and what the faculty needed to move student learning forward. They sought people who were sharper than those already in place.

This team approached the hiring process with a method that was hypothesis and data driven. The team studied how teaching and learning math was best accomplished in an urban setting. The two teachers on this team knew the strengths in the school, specifically the teachers who had some success with generating student interest in math. They also knew other urban math teachers who showed passion about teaching math.

They gathered some basic data on these teachers and found that these teachers made math instruction meaningful to real-life situations. They also discovered that these teachers incorporated math beyond the classroom: one started a robotics club, one ran a weekly math challenge for all students in the school, and another invited guest speakers to the classroom each semester to talk about how their work was connected to math. Their hypothesis was that teachers who make math meaningful for students and connect math beyond the classroom improve student learning and achievement. These were the teachers they sought.

TALENT VERSUS SKILL AND EFFORT

Natural talent is often regarded as a panacea for almost every success—especially in the workplace. Yet, other studies indicate that skill development supported by effort can have even greater benefits. In research in the area of talent versus skill, people with natural talent are regarded as superior. Someone with natural talent is a prize.

On the other hand, consider the skill development. Skill takes practice—deliberate practice that is planned and focused. To acquire skill, effort must be present.

In transforming an organization, while natural talent may be present, more often skill will need to be developed. Recognizing the talent within the members of the organization is a first step in designing organizational tasks. Small incremental change early enough in the process produces substantial results.

Considering both sides of the argument, was Pat naturally talented in transforming this school or was it his skill and effort that made the difference? The answer to both questions is "yes."

Natural talent in an organization is a gift, one that is encapsulated within the individual. Individual talent will only be as effective as the individual's ability to synergize with all the constituents of the organization. When the whole is greater than the sum of the parts, synergy is in place.

While Pat may have natural talents in transforming the organization, leadership is not about leading a party of one. All stakeholders have to be engaged. In this case, Pat knew he could not transform this situation by decisions he made in isolation. His talent may be described through his commitment to deliberate practice in bringing about a needed change.

TRANSFORMATION THROUGH DELIBERATE PRACTICE

Angela Duckworth (2016) identifies the basic requirements of deliberate practice as a component of grit:

- A clearly defined stretch goal
- Full concentration and effort

- Immediate and informative feedback
- Repetition with reflection and refinement (p. 137)

Pat used these requirements in transforming the learning and teaching of mathematics in this school.

Pat knew that the goal in this situation was more math learning for all students in more ways all of the time. While this goal was obvious to him, he could not reach this goal in isolation, no matter how talented he was. The first level of goal accomplishment was to get the right people in the room.

In bringing teachers on board, he inadvertently identified those who would not or could not believe in the goal. This happens. These teachers found a way to escape, while those who remained chose to move toward the goal.

While other aspects of organizational change were needed—on time performance, adherence to school procedures, parent involvement—full concentration and effort was made on improving teaching and learning of math. Realigning schedules, devoting professional development to this goal, creating a team for recruiting, and hiring needed teachers who could supplement current gaps in talent and skills contributed to a concentrated effort in making incremental changes.

Another aspect of deliberate practice in this situation was providing immediate and informative feedback. This started in small ways as teachers met in the weekly professional development sessions, also known as professional learning communities. This weekly focus on improving math included studies of effective math strategies, development of a school-wide problem-solving approach, teachers inviting colleagues into their classrooms to observe a focused skill development, and ways to provide feedback to students.

These initial meetings morphed into a 360-degree feedback program. This type of feedback ordinarily provides respondents with confidential and anonymous feedback from those working around them. In this case, teachers became more comfortable with one another and the focused development on student learning. Teachers did not view the feedback as competitive but rather as supportive.

Teachers took advantage of this feedback to develop a feedback tool that students used to evaluate their own learning as well as give insights to the teacher about what was happening in the classroom to promote more learning. Grade-level forms were established and each semester students participated in the feedback process. Teachers also committed to providing feedback to students using a three-step process: (1) identify what student did correctly; (2) identify one or two areas that needed improvement; and (3) suggest one way to make the improvement.

The weekly meetings allowed teachers to reflect on what was working and decide on next steps to transform the teaching and learning. The cyclical process mirroring action research led to more deliberate practice and eventually greater learning.

SURPASSING PERSONAL BEST

Pat's story had a happy ending—or beginning! "The team that became great didn't start off great—it learned how to produce extraordinary results" (Senge, 1990, p. 4). Transforming an organization is all about learning and growing and seeking common ground. This transformation took two years. At the end of the second year, the students in Pat's school showed the greatest improvement in mathematics in the entire district. Based on the normal curve equivalent scores, students showed three to four years of growth in a two-year period.

While this was the ultimate stretch goal, transformation of the climate and culture of the school also became a reality. Teachers learned that they had the talent and skills to make a difference and that united effort on their part made the goal achievable. They recognized the part they played in bringing about change and realized that this process was now possible for other needed change.

Leading others to transform the organization requires masterful leadership. This was once described as changing the tire on your bicycle while you are riding it. Nothing stops in the process while you take an organization apart and reassemble it.

Keller and Price, directors at McKinsey & Company, note that this kind of leadership must start at the top. They suggest four ways to lead successful transformation: (1) Be sure the transformation is meaningful; (2) model the change, mindset, and behavior you want to see; (3) build a strong and committed top team; (4) relentlessly pursue impact. All change begins with a change of mind.

> When [what you are deeply passionate about, what you can be best in the world at and what drives your economic engine] come together, not only does your work move toward greatness, but so does your life. For, in the end, it is impossible to have a great life unless it is a meaningful life. And it is very difficult to have a meaningful life without meaningful work. Perhaps, then, you might gain that rare tranquility that comes from knowing that you've had a hand in creating something of intrinsic excellence that makes a contribution. Indeed, you might even gain that deepest of all satisfactions: knowing that your short time here on this earth has been well spent, and that it mattered. (Collins, 2001, p. 210)

WHAT IF THEY DON'T?

Just because a leader has a position does not mean he or she should have that position. Don was new. He assumed a vice president position with the belief that he was the best candidate for the position. However, not all leaders are created equal.

Don came readymade with several assumptions. He knew it all. Any idea he presented was the best idea and was also what was best for everyone. His idea was the one that would make the change that the place always needed and never had—until he got here.

Don believed it was all about him. This became evident in staff meetings that he held monthly. He would regale others with his accomplishments and what he already knew, introduce his newest hires, and promote his chosen head his newly designed committees. He questioned those who questioned him and publicly chastised those who challenged his decisions. The monthly meetings started having fewer attendees and eventually the meetings became quarterly meetings and then annual meetings. Attendance remained low except for those new hires and the recently promoted.

To deal less with those who challenged his way of thinking, he assigned them to lower-level supervisory roles. He avoided gatherings of those he was hired to lead, and when he had to be present at these gatherings he spoke briefly and loudly to groups rather than individuals.

Accountability was totally lacking. When informational technology continued to fail in providing needed services to the employees, when the new block schedule presented course conflicts, when the instructional designer controlled course delivery with outdated methods, and when a change of policy impacting all employees and customers was initiated without previous notice, Don allowed the status quo to rule in favor of growth. No vision, except tunnel vision, existed.

Don was acting from a position—certainly not leading the organization to transformation. When the leader is focused on self, and surrounds the self with those who stroked his ego, ignoring the consumers and constituents, the organization is headed for disaster.

This is what happens when they don't. Don's organization no longer functions. It exists—but does not grow, or change, or lead others to grow or change. Don's organization resides in his mind and will stay there until Don realizes that no one is following his lead. Don cannot and will not lead with his party of one.

A comparison of Pat's leadership skills with Don's reveals how moving from good to great happens. Pat began with the end in mind—a quality education. Don was the end product. Pat sought teachers who complemented his own skill set—he hired up. Don promoted those who honored him. Pat transformed the organization through deliberate practice. He kept goals clearly in the view of all constituents; he drew out the talents of his staff to accomplish the goals and provided them with timely and specific feedback to enhance performance and refine efforts. Don maintained a status quo and hid behind the challenges that could have produced growth.

The position does not make the leader. The belief and commitment born of vision and mission and modeled by the leader results in *following the leader* to places the organization did not even realize existed.

REFERENCES

Collins, J. (2001). *Good to great: Why some companies make the leap and others don't*. New York, NY: Harper Business.

Davis, F. (2014, September 26). *Tips for schools interested in restorative justice*. Edutopia. Retrieved from https://www.edutopia.org/blog/restorative-justice-tips-for-schools-fania-davis

Duckworth, A. (2016). *Grit: The power of passion and perseverance*. New York: Scribner.

Grange, P. (2013). The bluestone review: A review of culture and leadership in Australian Olympic Swimming. Retrieved from http://resources.news.com.au/files/2013/02/19/1226580/881151-swimming-australia-culture-review.pdf

Kotter, J. (2012, September 27). The key to changing organizational culture. Retrieved from http://www.forbes.com/sites/johnkotter/2012/09/27/the-key-to-changing-organizational-culture/#580f0dbe7238

Senge, P. M. (1990). *The fifth discipline: The art & practice of the learning organization*. New York, NY: Doubleday.

Thorsborne, M., & Blood, P. (2013). *Implementing restorative practices in schools: A practical guide to transforming school communities*. Philadelphia, PA: Jessica Kingsley Publishers.

Chapter 12

A Platform for Spreading Ideas That Work

> *Culture does not change because we desire to change it. Culture changes when the organization is transformed; the culture reflects the realities of people working together every day.*
>
> —Frances Hesselbein

A fundamental disposition for transforming an organization is the realization that the organization must constantly become more of what it intends to be. The mission, the vision, the hopes for the organization form the road map to "arrive where we started" (T. S. Eliot).

Responses will be guided by the disposition to believe that all change begins with a change of mind, that connectedness is the goal, that participantship—not leadership or followership—is the ethical imperative. It is everyone's responsibility to do good work at work, to surpass yesterday's best as a measure of organizational learning.

The skill to synergize needs the disposition that no one is working as hard as he or she can to fail and to believe that humans have a fundamental desire to belong to something larger than themselves. This chapter examines the dispositions leaders need to transform the organization. To lead with others to transform the organization means being disposed to relationships and to connectedness—to each other, to the past and present, to the future—and the belief that sharing information is power.

TAKE THIS JOB AND . . .

Troy Smith and Jan Rivkin have defined a job as a "bundle of tasks that have been clumped together." If that is the case, then what is the bundle of tasks that make up leading the organization? One of the tasks is to design the leadership of the organization so it is done *with* its members, not to them, not in spite of them, not aside from them. Leading with others begins with personal experience and ends with the experiences others will have of the organization.

Individuals have serious requirements of the organizations in which they carve out a quarter of their 168 hours a week. For those in charge, that percentage can reach half or even more. Those whose lives are affected by the organization, even if they don't work in it, have legitimate expectations of the organization as well—their families, churches, schools, stores, banks, and so on.

So, the basic disposition of the organizational leader has to do with the expectations of internal and external stakeholders. The expectations of internal stakeholders—the employees, workers, teachers, accountants—are pretty straightforward. They want to have some part to play in decisions that will affect their work lives. It is a mismeme that money or salary or benefits or other rewards are the highest motivator. Instead, in the 2014 survey of employee job satisfaction and engagement, respectful treatment of employees and a trusting relationship of employees and supervisors trumped benefits, compensation, and job security (Society for Human Resource Management, 2015).

The same survey reviewed employee engagement to learn that relationships with co-workers, contribution to the organization's goals, and the meaningfulness of the job were important to the engagement of workers in the enterprise. In 2016, compensation moved up in the survey but engagement continued to be sourced by relationships with co-workers, on-the-job opportunities to use skills and abilities, and meaningful work (Society for Human Resource Management, 2016).

External stakeholders, while not necessarily a part of the organization, have an interest in the outcomes of the organization—health benefits, safe flights, an education that prepares for the next level of accomplishment, financial security, product satisfaction, and on-time arrival. Without external stakeholders, the organization lacks purpose. The leader is consciously aware of its external stakeholders and how the organization is meeting their needs and that their needs serve the organization.

WHAT'S LOVE GOT TO DO WITH IT?

Learning about what employees want from their organizations—relationships and meaningful work—and what organizations need from employees—engagement and productivity—points to a new role for leaders: developing a culture that centers on subtler and more important tasks. Senge (2006) describes leaders as designers, teachers, and stewards. Each of these roles carries certain dispositions with them that can be hallmarks of leading with others.

The designer cares whether the organization actually does what it says it does. The designer anticipates potential problems and deals with them ahead of time. Design does not take place in a vacuum. Design thinking requires learning from the end users of the product. Design implies making changes. The well-disposed leader knows that all change begins with a change of mind, that all things are created twice—once in the imagination and a second time in reality (Covey, 2004).

The steward is the visionary. The leader exemplifies stewardship for the well-being of the employees. The steward provides opportunity for creativity and innovation, for learning and self-actualization. The steward strives for professional excellence in both products and services, has a clear vision of the organization, and instills that vision in all stakeholders.

The leader as teacher serves as a mentor for the organization. The leader knows how others learn and inspires them to keep learning, thus developing the will to learn. The teacher defines reality for the organization, with reality being the practical matters. By acting as designer, steward, and teacher, the leader joins vision and practicality and brings together ideas and dreams (Senge, 2006).

Covey references *live, love, learn,* and *leave a legacy* as cornerstones of effective people and, by extension, effective organizations. The cornerstone of *love* represents relationships, that desired component of employee engagement of the Society for Human Resource Management Survey (2015, 2016). All stakeholders in the enterprise must realize that they belong to something larger than themselves and in that belonging have something to contribute.

Effective leadership then must necessarily go beyond individual success and achievement to include the imperative to develop a learning community whose members recognize that together they are building the future. Margaret Wheatley (1999) reminds us that "relationships are primary" (p. 69) and that is why the leader who leads with others is the organization's steward (Senge, 2006) and servant (Greenleaf, 1977), not its master.

Love, according to Daft (2007), is a potent form of leadership that becomes a way of living and actually has power. As such, this power improves performance, helps to connect others, is enriching, and contributes to an environment that permits risk, improves learning, and promotes growth (van Dierendonck & Patterson, 2010). Another antidote to authority by position, Deft's concept of what love has to do with it is based on treating others with dignity and respect, inspiring them to higher levels of service, work, and purpose. Manz, Anand, Joshi, and Manz (2008) believed this idea was fundamental to ethical leadership; Bakke (2005) believed it made followers (participants) a first priority.

The *learn* cornerstone represents the basic human characteristic of wanting, even needing, to be challenged. Taking the teaching role of leadership believes that others grow from learning. Peter Senge's learning organization relies on the leader as teacher and as the lead learner. As an example, he cites Greg Merten (2002) that "learning is the very source of leading" (p. 333).

In his speech at the Dimensions of Leadership Conference in 2002, Merten elaborated with a claim that lacking a goal, a desired result, is a leadership issue. And further, that learning, which he calls the source of leadership, focuses on learning about ourselves, our relationships, and how to operate organizationally that can produce a desired result.

Learning to take people with you means learning first what is important to them and making sure it happens. Organizational transformation requires leading with others who care as much about the organization as the leaders or owners do.

Having meaningful work was noted as a high-ranking condition of employee engagement. The well-dispositioned leader believes in doing good work at work. One form of good work, arguably intangible, is being oriented toward dignity, choosing those actions and participating in those activities that enhance dignity rather than diminish it, that develop capability rather than dependence.

Enhancing dignity means that all aspects of the life of the organization are considered for their role in transforming stakeholders from dependent to independent and ultimately to interdependent. Transforming leadership helps individuals move from conforming to norms to internalizing those norms. Organizational behavior is transformed as a result of moving from interactions that protect the status quo to those that are growth producing. Such individual and organizational transformation moves the enterprise forward to remaining true to its original purposes and intended outcomes.

WHAT DO I HAVE TO DO?

When Donna successfully acquired a grant for professional development, one of the conditions was that the entire staff had to participate. As always, some members did not want to participate. Donna began an abductive process (Shuttleworth, 2008) of filtering through all the reasons why that might be so. She used design thinking to build up the cadre of those who would participate. When nearly all agreed, she was in a position to return to the recalcitrant member: What do I have to do to help you become part of this endeavor?

Making it matter made the difference. Faced with the fact that all others would be included, it was difficult for a recalcitrant member to hold out and remain aloof from the endeavor.

An orientation toward connectedness represents the willingness to choose the things that draw people together rather than separate them or discriminate against them. It also means including people in decision making and in creating the future of their choice. It further means connecting people to their past, including them in their present, and recognizing them as bridges to the future. Connecting means sharing—activities, experiences, opportunities, meaning, and understanding as well as money, time, information.

Simple assent to these ideas is probably possible. Their complexity lies in the hard work of making them a reality. What these principles mean to the various stakeholders in the enterprise is juxtaposed against how they see these values played out in everyday reality.

LEAVE A LEGACY

The cornerstone of *leave a legacy* points to external stakeholders who, like internal stakeholders, want relationships. Businesses that change branding found themselves reverting to the "old" ways because external customers missed the legacy. An example is Tropicana's new branding that had to be dropped, or the local restaurant that tried to modernize and was forced to reopen under *old* management because customers relished their legacy. JCPenney also comes to mind.

Deciding to do away with sales, Penney introduced "month-long values" that would eliminate the accoutrements of specials and so-called reductions. Instead, consumers could rest assured they were always getting the best price, period. Unfortunately, customers hated the idea and criticized JCP's implementation. The company suffered a drop in profits and strong negative consumer feedback. JCP's then president, Michael Francis, announced his resignation soon thereafter. Unfortunately, for JCP, consumers want sales, and they wanted their coupons! Consumers loved the original legacy, and the company deserted it with negative consequences.

All engaged in the enterprise recognize that their efforts to act with excellence, dignity, and connectedness guarantee the existence of these principles in the future. The legacy is an enterprise where learning takes place, grounded in excellence, dignity, and connectedness, and whose stakeholders, clients, and customers reveal these principles in their businesses, families, and personal lives.

Research affirms organizational effectiveness that results from broad participative action based on vision and mission. Systems theory has become a given. Participation in decision making has become a sine qua non of quality organizations. The learning leader builds community, a concept that has remained largely unchanged for several decades, (Sergiovanni, 2000); draws people together through consensus, team building, and participative management (Wynn & Guditus, 1984); and leads with others to develop a learning organization that fulfills its mission by remaining true to its purposes by constantly seeking and learning new ways to accomplish it (Senge, 2006; Bolman & Deal, 2013).

Leaders prepare for the future by taking an active role in creating it. As internal and external constituencies become better informed, more involved, and politicized, competing values create added demands. Creating a preferred future requires knowledge, skills, and dispositions for finding common ground among stakeholders' competing demands.

The learning leader must be an entrepreneur who actively accepts the ups and downs of organizational development and seeks out disparate stakeholders to encourage them to get aboard with their self-interest, feelings, and experiences, to be willing to plunge to the depths of apparent chaos, to own up to the part they play in the "mess" that must be dealt with. From these initial steps, the learning leader helps the organization's constituencies rise to the heights where they can consider the future they prefer to live in, to use the teaching role of leadership to help stakeholders dialogue about real choices and to take responsibility for creating the future all would like to live in (Weisbord & Janoff, 2015).

Basing such entrepreneurship on lasting principles addresses the globalization of economics and the immediacy of communication. As such, a lack of principled behavior is distressfully obvious. Individuals and organizations are reportedly voicing concern for and taking action against behavior that compromises the integrity of individuals and the environment on a global scale.

Increased accountability is the result of increased scrutiny and demands for responsible behavior (Naisbitt, 1994). For such accountability and responsible self-direction to become commonplace, rather than heroic, principled behavior must become routine. A deliberate orientation to excellence, dignity, and connectedness offers opportunities for reflection and growth among internal and external stakeholders. These are powerful, practical tools for creating a future in which such principles will be available to all and a legacy worthy of the enterprise.

Leaders who continually enhance their own and others' knowledge, skills, and dispositions for strategic, instructional, organizational, and political/community leadership see the result in quality. Deliberately considering ways to create an environment in which these principles are practiced daily will form an important component of leadership programs.

Learning leaders, designers, lead with the authority that comes from a personal mission rather than waiting for a public position of leadership. Leading self to act on excellence, dignity, and connectedness precedes leading others to such actions. Leaders understand that personal leadership and personal mastery precede leading others so they can find areas within their spheres of influence where principled behavior is needed. They will reflect on what is lacking in the present and strategize to create conditions that will produce in the future what is lacking in the present. Developments in scientific fields will continue to influence the management and leadership of organizations.

Leaders uncover and discover their own missions that brought them to seek and/or accept leadership positions in the enterprise. They must learn ways to keep the mission constantly in mind and how to learn of others' missions. The result of this knowledge, skill, and disposition will be that the mission becomes the "strange attractor" toward which all actions and behaviors tend over time.

As purveyors of learning, leaders must know how to audit organizational health, position the mission as a product in the minds of stakeholders, build high performance through team work, and add value to organizational output—citizens with marketable skills and the disposition to make a return on the investment made in them.

Parallel to developing entrepreneurial leadership, leaders must be able to impart the need for entrepreneurship, particularly by providing the stakeholders with the capacity to consider themselves a product to be marketed, positioned, and profited from. Considerations of this sort develop dispositions toward connectedness, drawing together those with resources to share, those whose use of the resources will benefit those who share it, those whose profitability depend on the skill of future consumers and constituents.

MOVING FORWARD

While many think about the need to change the way we do business, few are thinking through the complexity of that change to the simplicity on the other side. That simplicity can be as fundamental as becoming more so, taking action, and judging those actions against criteria of excellence, dignity, and connectedness. Research affirms effectiveness resulting from broad participative action based on a mission and vision.

As today's leaders search for a desired future for their organizations and communities, they need a framework for acting and for judging those actions so they can eliminate barriers and build strategies that support and enhance effective behaviors at all levels. Professional development that continually enhances knowledge, skills, and dispositions for strategic, instructional, organizational, and political/community leadership must be augmented with consideration of lasting principles in which to ground that organization and the components of a supportive environment in which to deliver it.

WHAT IF THEY DON'T?

Organizational transformation failure is more common than success. McKinsey's survey of the success of transformational efforts of nearly 3,000 executives found the failure rate to be more than 60 percent, and a *Harvard Business Review* study found that more than 70 percent of transformation efforts failed. Many organizational leaders want transformation to happen quickly, with minimal effort, and outside of themselves. And yet, the place leaders need to begin the transformation is with themselves (Carruci, 2016).

For organizational transformation to take place, connectedness is the goal, and participantship—not leadership or followership—is the ethical imperative. When connectedness and participation are lacking, transformation is not possible.

Within four years, three capable, talented, and highly effective professors were hired—all for the same job—to prepare future teachers. These women had served as elementary or high school science teachers, were principals in schools, and worked in district level education positions. Each had received awards for innovative teaching or science study projects. They acquired a high level of expertise based on their own experiences as well as their academic background. So what was the problem?

These women were entering an environment of walls—not bridges. They knew too much, had great ideas to offer, and were able to see through the culture of expediency and the cult of personality that encased this organization.

The first hired was Anna. Her weekly commute of two hours did not diminish her enthusiasm for working with future elementary teachers, especially in the field of science. She also had an exceptional talent for incorporating mobile technology into her classes. She was dismissed after two years in the position—apparently she was not *involved* enough to meet the "expectations" of the department. She moved on to lead educators in science inquiry, teacher education, and technology integration in classrooms at another institution of higher education.

Mary Louise followed the next year. Like Anna, her experiences were vast with scientific inquiry and in critical and creative thinking in Maker Space and developing global leaders and scholars. The classes she taught actively engaged learners and connected real-life learning in curriculum development. The potential teachers she taught worked hard, laughed often, and prepared lessons that were immediately useful in local schools. The department dismissed her within one year as a non–team player. She went on to become the chief learning officer of an educational enterprise that builds innovative partnerships with higher education institutions, programs, and faculty.

Then there was Susanna. Like her two predecessors, experience at all levels of education, including instructional coaching and collaborative leadership, made her ideal for preparing future educators. While her strong science background was certainly one of her outstanding skills, Susanna had just led her previous high school to *U.S. News & World Report* silver performance status. She had a talent for closing opportunity gaps. During her one-year stay, she worked with students in developing writing skills by meeting one on one with students to help them revise their writing assignments. She was dismissed with an acknowledgment that the department really needed someone with more innovative ideas. She went on to another higher education institution and continued preparing future educators in scientific inquiry.

Certainly, these women were focused on transforming not only the organization but transforming lives beyond the organization. The organization, however, lacked connectedness and participation.

These women were regarded as place fillers—until their competence became such an overwhelming contrast to the efficacy mode that was in operation. In a note sent to the provost, Mary Louise reported: "You have a real problem in the Department. There is a level of complacency that I have not experienced before. People who work hard are criticized—and worse for it. In K-12 environments we call it bullying. Senior members of the department are afraid to speak up for fear of retaliation. Please do something about it" (personal communication, August 24, 2014).

This is what happens when they don't. Not only does the organization suffer but those for whom the organization exists—the outside stakeholders—are robbed of opportunities of transformation.

Transformed organizations require connectedness and participation among all the members. The organization is interdependent, with effective leaders enacting intervention strategies that promote a living and active vision and mission, with members sharing a will to learn while promoting self-efficacy, group efficiency, use of time as a resource, and acknowledgment of challenges and problems as opportunities to transform the world.

REFERENCES

Bakke, D. W. (2005). *Joy at work: A revolutionary approach to fun on the job.* Seattle, WA: PVG.

Bolman, L., & Deal, T. (2013). *Reframing organizations: Artistry, choice and leadership*, 5th ed. San Francisco, CA: Jossey-Bass.

Carruci, R. (2016). Organizations can't change if leaders can't change with them. Retrieved from https://hbr.org/2016/10/organizations-cant-change-if-leaders-cant-change-with-them

Covey, S. R. (2004). *The 7 habits of highly effective people: Powerful lessons in personal change.* New York, NY: Free Press.

Daft, R. L. (2007). *The leadership experience.* Boston, MA: South-Western College.

Greenleaf, R. (1977). *Servant leadership.* Mahwah, NJ: Paulist Press.

Manz, C. C., Anand, V., Joshi, M., & Manz, K. (2008). Executive leadership: A theoretical interpretation of the tensions between corruption and virtuous leaders. *Leadership Quarterly* 19, 385–392.

Merten, G. (2002). Dimensions of Leadership Conference for the Leadership Development Academy of the Graduate School, Washington, D.C., November 25. Retrieved from http://faculty-staff.ou.edu/H/Lawrence.Hynson-1//FtSill07/Greg_Merten_Speecha.pdf

Naisbitt, J. (1994). *Global paradox*. New York, NY: William Morrow.

Senge, P. (2006). *The fifth discipline: The art and practice of the learning organization*. New York, NY: Currency Doubleday.

Sergiovanni, T. J. (2000). *The lifeworld of leadership: Creating culture, community, and personal meaning in our schools. The Jossey-Bass education series*. San Francisco, CA: Jossey-Bass.

Shuttleworth, M. (2008, July 23). Abductive reasoning. Retrieved from https://explorable.com/abductive-reasoning

Society for Human Resource Management. (2015, April 28). 2015 employee job satisfaction and engagement: Optimizing organizational culture for success. Retrieved from https://www.shrm.org/hr-today/trends-and-forecasting/research-and-surveys/pages/job-satisfaction-and-engagement-report-optimizing-organizational-culture-for-success.aspx

Society for Human Resource Management. (2016, April 18). 2016 employee job satisfaction and engagement: Revitalizing a changing workforce. Retrieved from https://www.shrm.org/hr-today/trends-and-forecasting/research-and-surveys/Documents/2016-Employee-Job-Satisfaction-and-Engagement-Report-Executive-Summary.pdf

van Dierendonck, D., & Patterson, K. (Eds). (2010). *Servant leadership: Developments in theory and research*. New York, NY: Palgrave Macmillan.

Weisbord, M., & Janoff, S. (2015). *Lead more, control less*. San Francisco, CA: Berrett-Koehler.

Wheatley, M. (1999). *Leadership and the new science: Discovering order in a chaotic world.* San Francisco, CA: Berrett-Koehler.

Wynn, R., & Guditus, C. W. (1984). *Team management: Leadership by consensus*. Columbus, OH: Merrill.

REFLECTION—PART IV: LEADING WITH OTHERS TO TRANSFORM THE ORGANIZATION

Vision/Mission

1. How are others invited to share their visions of the organization?
2. What aspects of the current culture provide the greatest opportunity? The greatest challenge?
3. What is the preferred future for the organization? Who envisions that future?
4. How do dignity, connectedness, and excellence relate to transforming your organization?
5. How does the mission of your colleagues contribute to the mission of the organization?
6. What story describes your organization surpassing its personal best?

Time Management
1. What is the greatest area of growth in your organization in the past year? Five years? Ten years?
2. What task have you delegated and how did you delegate it?
3. What is the meaningful work of your organization?

Desire to Learn
1. What holds people back from surpassing their personal best?
2. What was the greatest success the organization experienced?
3. Think of one of your colleagues. What is the connection between the colleague's goals and the goals of the organization? What is the connection between the colleague's needs and the needs of the organization?
4. How do the talented, skillful, and determined move your organization to greatness?

Self-Talk
1. What signs decorate common spaces in the organization? Who puts them there?
2. How do outsiders describe your organization?
3. What story of engagement describes your organization?

Problem Solving
1. Describe how the structure of your organization influences the behavior of the group.
2. To what are employees most committed?
3. Where is the level of greatest compliance?

Part V

THE FUTURE OF LEADERSHIP

Having considered the necessity of leading self, leading others to lead themselves, and leading with others to transform the organization, we look to the future of leadership and how leadership will develop as an investment for the future.

This part considers leadership as action rather than position. Leaders who will be worthy of the name will operate from an abundance mentality. Decision making through problem solving will characterize the role of leaders—all those involved in the transformation of the organization. These leaders will move forward in learning, using neuroscience findings to promote actions grounded in brain research and assuming responsibility as a way of being for the organization. Collective, lateral, and integral leadership will characterize the future of leadership.

Chapter 13

Leadership Is Action, Not Position

T.S. Eliot (1943) lets us know that the only way to learn about life is by exploring life. Organizational transformation, like the journey of a thousand miles, begins with a single step, leading self. Finding one's personal/professional mission is foundational to serving the mission of the organization. The goal of organizational transformation is to become more of what the organization claims for itself: to provide a quality product, one that is based on and grounded in lasting principles and delivered in a supportive environment. By way of reflection, no Sherpa goes to the mountain top alone. Even if the guide is the only one who knows the way, the point of being a Sherpa is to help others reach the heights.

This chapter examines leadership as action. No position makes a leader. Leadership is earned and has followers.

WHAT DOES IT MEAN TO TRANSFORM THE ORGANIZATION?

Organizational transformation means different things to different people. Some have a frame of mind that says "if it ain't broke, don't fix it!" Others are all for the change as long as it does not affect them or what they do, a variation on nimby—not in my back yard. Others, like Robert Kennedy, see things as they might be and ask why not? The transformation that is considered in this chapter is based on a Salada Tea Tag, which claimed, "as we get older, we don't change; we become more so"! The transformed organization is more so—more vision centered, more aligned with the vision and mission, more of what it purports to be. More time is spent to produce continuous improvement, more problems are solved based on the fundamental character of the organization, not on expedience or profit at any cost. The members become more so as well—they are more informed, more involved, more caring, more attuned to the imperative of continuous improvement.

To transform the organization means that from the top down—and the bottom up—the vision and mission are known, are evident, and are the source of action. The urge is to be better, the focus is others—the consumer, the end user of the service—the work is future oriented, the action is service oriented, and "how can I help?" is the individual and organizational mantra.

If transformation is understood this way, then the need to lead with others becomes obvious. Everyone has the responsibility, including those who are not in charge! You don't need a title to be a leader, remember? Collective thought is individuals with a desire to learn and who contribute to a learning organization. Their purpose leads to engagement. Their facility with deconstructive feedback asks, doesn't tell, and protects against the "didn't you hear what I said?" syndrome. Participantship at every level possible is standard operating procedure: all this without the Pollyanna view that it will be easy.

LEADERSHIP ACTION

That is why leading self with a mission and vision, time management skill, a problem-solving frame of mind, a will to learn, and goal-oriented, positive self-talk are essential to organization-wide needs and activities. As mentioned in chapter 1, there are many leadership characteristics; some related to personal qualities, some to relationships, some to organizational leadership. The same is true of leadership actions. There is no one set of actions that, if performed, defines a person as a leader.

Standards for educational leadership are an example of the variety of leadership activities, in the form of performances that lead to educational effectiveness. The Baldridge Award (NIST/BPEP, 2016), the nation's only presidential award for performance excellence, offers criteria, assessments, tools, and training to help organizations improve. Similar to the educational accreditation standards, Baldridge standards also refer to performances at all levels of leadership: organizational performance management that increases value to customers and stakeholders and contributes to organizational sustainability; overall managerial effectiveness and capabilities; and organizational and personal learning.

WE SHALL NOT CEASE FROM EXPLORATION

Accreditation agencies for businesses, schools, health care, and laboratories have a variety of measures of performance, quality of product, or quality of service. In each case, the starting point is the vision, mission, and fundamental goals of the organization, its purpose. Exploring the entity through evaluation renews the commitment to the vision and mission. To apply the concept of evaluation to leading self means reviewing one's personal mission, its alignment with the mission of the organization. As a learning leader, finding a way to make the mission obvious and relevant to co-workers, colleagues, and employees contributes to the organization's faithfulness to its mission.

Vision and Mission

Dr. Covey speaks of moving from the mission to the moment. This step of the exploration requires being able to use the mission as the rationale for decisions, actions, outcomes. The responsibility for making the mission obvious and evident in everyday action becomes the norm of a mission-based culture. One way of thinking was explained by Adriaan Bekman, in *The Mystery of Leadership* (2014). Bekman claims that the vision for an organization is exhibited by striving toward something special. Continuing in the striving with attention can function like a self-fulfilling prophecy. Something happens that, although not originally sought, seems like a valued objective anyway—what the striving was for in the first place. Even though what happens may differ somewhat from what was originally imagined, the striving results in something related to the goal of the striving. Something will ultimately manifest itself as a potential answer.

Time

Adhering to the alignment of action with the mission leads to growth in time management skill—using time to forward the mission, keeping the main thing the main thing (Covey, 1989). The awareness of how time is used by the learning leader is the basis for helping others in the organization use time to integrate the mission into daily actions. Leading self means acting in a way that models effective time management so team members see day-to-day behavior that is congruent with the belief in the vision and mission. Awareness of the vision and mission become common in the organization. Goals are specific, communication takes priority, and personal mastery is the key to following plans that promote the mission.

Will to Learn

Finding ways to keep the vision and mission uppermost and influential in everyday action requires going beyond the status quo. The constant question has to be about how to get better, that is, no matter how good the present is, the future must get better. Improvement is a light switch—it is either on or off: there is no dimmer switch. A culture of *kaizen* must be the order of the day. Finding out what can be better and how to make it better requires a desire to learn. Leading self means having the will to learn. The need to learn is a given; the will to learn is a choice.

Technology doubles knowledge yearly. As a result, strategic knowledge management has become essential to organizations. This is the relation of learning to time. Productivity can be measured in hours to learn. There is a cost to ignorance. The learning organization comprises leaders who value learning themselves and who facilitate learning among the members. Organizational transformation is the result of a vision of what could be, the use of time to create a product based on possibility, and the continual learning to enhance capability.

Human beings are wired to learn. Electronically generated images of the brain show that learning something new produces brain action that appears as lightened areas of the brain. Those who already know do not have lightened areas in their brains. The takeaway is that learning lights up the brain. Further information about learning indicates that dendrites continue to develop when learning continues. The message is to keep the brain lit up, to keep learning.

Self-Talk

Really? Is talking to oneself not psychotic? It can be when misused or pushed to extremes, a source of painful rumination or even psychosis. On the other hand, self-talk can also provide the distance of detachment to become an observer of one's own life. Actually, inner talk can be an effective tool leading to success. Furthermore, talking to oneself is common and has actually been found to be helpful.

Pamela Weintraub, a consulting editor for *Psychology Today*, calls self-talk the voice of reason (2015). Citing psychologists, she claims that addressing the self in the first or third person flips a switch in the cerebral cortex, the center of thought, and another in the amygdala, the seat of fear, moving closer to or further from a sense of self and emotional intensity.

The result of gaining psychological distance enhances self-control, allows clear thinking, and improves performance. The language switch also minimizes the rumination that breeds anxiety and depression. Negative self-talk is of more concern even though it is a vestige of the flight-or-fight mechanism in the brain. A release from negative thoughts increases perspective and focus and facilitates planning for the future.

For the learning leader, self-talk can be a prelude to personal action, to communicating with others, to creating the mental and emotional conditions for improvement. The external version might be a roundtable brainstorming session with others. The hard thing is developing the personal mastery to overcome negativity in self-talk and transform it into reflection and positivity, an abundance mentality.

Weintraub cites scientists who say the inner voice begins in childhood and remains a lifelong companion, intimate and constant, actual thought. When asked by Theaetetus to define thought, Socrates replied, "the talk which the soul has with itself." When dealing with strong emotions, taking a step back and becoming a detached observer can help. It is so easy to give advice to others. It is not so easy to take the same advice. However, research shows that those who engage in self-talk using their first names, in effect, are distancing themselves from the self, right in the moment, and that helps them perform.

For the learning leader, self-talk has to master the negative self-talk of a scarcity mentality and take on the characteristics of what Covey termed an *abundance mentality*, presented in his *7 Habits of Highly Effective People*. People with a scarcity mentality have a very difficult time sharing recognition and credit, power or profit—even with those who help in the production. They also have a very hard time being genuinely happy for the successes of other people—even, and sometimes especially, members of their own family or close friends and associates.

It's almost as if something is being taken from them when someone else receives special recognition or a windfall gain or has remarkable success or achievement. Although they may verbally express happiness for others' success, inwardly they are eating their hearts out. Their sense of worth comes from being compared, and someone else's success, to some degree, means their failure. Only so many people can be "A" students; only one person can be "number one." To "win" simply means to "beat." It's difficult for people with a scarcity mentality to be members of a complementary team. They look on differences as signs of insubordination and disloyalty.

AN ABUNDANCE MENTALITY

An abundance mentality is a disposition that flows out of a deep inner sense of personal worth and security. It is the disposition that believes there is plenty out there and enough to spare for everybody. It results in sharing of prestige, of recognition, of profits, of decision making. It opens possibilities, options, alternatives, and creativity; it takes joy, satisfaction, and fulfillment and turns it outward, appreciating the uniqueness, the inner direction, the proactive nature of others. It recognizes the unlimited possibilities for positive interactive growth and development (Covey, 2004).

Helping others lead themselves to a disposition of an abundance mentality and positive self-talk does not happen by correction or figurative finger wagging: "Why don't you ever?" "How come you never?" Instead, the personal mastery that facilitates a teaching role of leadership simply provides an alternative view. Franco's story is illustrative.

Franco was a division chair. At a regular meeting, the scuttle butt was that one of the members, Boyd, deserved to be fired because he simply did not pull his own weight. The mumbling became conversation that stymied the discussion that needed to be held. Franco allowed the topic to continue for a bit and remarked that what the group was saying seemed out of character since Boyd had been so generous in serving on a fund-raiser.

Someone in the group remembered something else and offered agreement. "Yeah, he helped me, too, when I needed some extra time for a report." That initiated further remembering about other good things without Franco having to tell everyone that "we don't do that around here." Instead, further discussion led to some positive suggestions about how to help Boyd over the rough spot he was in. An abundance mentality on Franco's part led to sharing of positive impressions.

It doesn't always work that way, but that's a possible way for negativity to turn around. The learning leader with a will to learn how to use self-talk for personal and organizational benefit may use the approach learned from Carol Dweck's *Mindset* and Peter Senge's mental models. Dweck's work proposes that replacing a fixed mindset with a growth mindset can lead to success and happiness. Senge's concept of fixed mental models is a reminder not to believe everything we think! "The mind is its own place, and in itself can make a heaven of hell, a hell of heaven" (Milton, 1667).

PROBLEM SOLVING

Gina Cajucom is the CEO and founder of Problem Solving Leader found at http://www.problemsolvingleader.com/. Gina is an international leadership development expert who helps firms' leaders improve their problem-solving and decision-making skills. Her research indicated that 75 percent of employees who responded did not feel that their senior management was fully prepared to make important decisions. Likewise, over a quarter of senior managers lack the necessary skills or expertise to make effective decisions.

Assessing problem-solving expertise means having a rationale and context for decision making, having the necessary tools to make a decision about a problem, working with a team to solve problems, seeking different perspectives about the issue, and having knowledge of various problem-solving techniques.

Learning leaders have learned that there is more than one way to solve a problem, that communication is necessary throughout the problem-solving process, and that implementing a solution may have to take place in stages. These leaders are disposed to see problems as opportunities for continuous improvement, that solving a problem is creating the conditions that produce in the future what is lacking in the present.

Problem solving is the essence of what leaders do. All of life is problem solving. From the youngest child struggling to open a bottle to the oldest adult struggling to open a bottle, solving a problem can be a source of great satisfaction. Leaders solving problems need to use the LEADER approach to solving problems. Mary Ann Jacobs and Bruce Cooper (2015) provided six steps in the LEADER process: (1) *L*ook at the problem; (2) *E*xamine what is known; (3) *A*cquire new knowledge; (4) *D*evise a plan; (5) *E*xecute the plan; (6) *R*epeat the steps as needed.

Look at the Problem

The learning leader subscribes to the need to look at the problem and state it accurately. Einstein is quoted (Passuello, n.d.) as having said that if he had one hour to save the world he would spend fifty-five minutes defining the problem and only five minutes finding the solution.

The takeaway is to step back, invest time and effort to improve our understanding of the problem. Supposedly, Einstein was suggesting that the quality of the solution will be in direct proportion to the accuracy of problem definition in the first place.

Examine What You Know

The leaders' will to learn operates in this stage of problem solving. It is necessary to engage team members in the process to investigate causes, origins, and circumstances of the problem. If the problem is vague, the task is to seek specificity and to consider what is not known about the problem. Team members have to be curious about the problem. The challenge is to seek simplicity if the problem seems complex. It is also necessary to examine what others know about the problem by seeking multiple perspectives and perceptions—leading others to lead themselves—so varying facets can be illuminated. To transform the organization, it is essential to seek the perceptions of those most affected by the problem.

Learning leaders gather facts and others' perceptions about the problem. They also attach a problem to the goal of continual improvement, the transformation of the organization into more of what it claims to be. With others, learning leaders ask and answer: in what ways will the solution to this problem affect the effectiveness or the functioning of the organization?

Acquire Knowledge

Acquiring knowledge assumes there are many solutions, not just one. Acquiring knowledge leads to examining what others have done with similar problems. The leader uses the research that is out there to gain greater knowledge about the problem. The will to learn how others have addressed similar situations contributes to designing a possible plan of action.

Self-talk enters the process of acquiring knowledge. Negative self-talk makes demands on cognitive processing while positive statements may help find the intended goal of solving the problem. If the problem can be phrased in the form of a question after considering the research, it may engage the brain's capacity to answer questions. This suggestion for creativity gives the brain time to work in the background, even while sleeping, to act on the problem.

Devise a Plan

Leaders with an aptitude for problem solving have the ability to analyze, diagnose, and deal with problems effectively. Whether the problem is linear and "tame" or nonlinear and "wicked," adept problem solvers have a natural propensity to discover and help lead others to solutions.

The leaders of tomorrow must learn to be collaborative problem-solving facilitators, instead of solitary master problem solvers. Problem-solving ability is a multifaceted competency that uses other skills, including conceptual thinking, planning and organization, and creativity. These contribute to making a plan of action to address the problem.

Pólya (1945) mentions that there are many reasonable ways to solve problems. The skill to choose an appropriate strategy is best learned by solving many problems. Some of the strategies Pólya recommends for devising a plan are chunking and hunking, looking for patterns. Problem-solving leaders look for problems similar to their own or more general than their own. They research how others devised a method to solve a similar problem and devise a plan using this information.

The *Apollo 13* team devised a plan to get home to Earth. Those who clean up oil spills devised a way to capture the lost oil. The inventor of post-it notes wanted a way to mark the pages of his hymn book. The inventor of Velcro saw how thistles worked and devised a plan to solve the problem of holding on to things in gravity-free spaceships.

Execute the Plan

To execute the plan, the leader should be clear about the desired outcome. So often, there are unintended consequences that negate the work that has gone into the process. Self-talk about what will be better or different when the plan is implemented will point the way to the desired outcome. The steps of planning the objectives will have helped to gain clarity about what success looks like. The implementation process can then effectively engage others in the process: those who care and will benefit from the solution; those who can contribute and help evaluate the solutions; those who have the knowledge and expertise to help execute and evaluate effectively. In the end, the question is a simple one: did the plan deliver the desired and intended outcomes?

Repeat as Necessary

What's next now that a problem has been defined and a plan designed and implemented? The evaluation component needs to be followed with monitoring. Are there any unintended consequences of the executed plan? Are there some steps that must be returned to and redone? Now is the time for considering the transformation of the organization. Was the problem a real problem or was it a symptom of a problem? Does it recur? What is the source of the problem? What data need to be collected to determine whether the problem continues in a different form?

Growing in leadership means paying close attention to the consequences of leadership decisions. Continual progress and improvement means considering the future and having access to the data that produce the necessary knowledge about what caused the problem in the first place, what resolved it, how to prevent it in the future. Day-to-day leadership that deals gracefully with the inevitable challenges of the job boosts team morale and group efficacy.

REFERENCES

Bekman, A. (2014, November). *The mystery of leadership*. IMO Academy. Retrieved from http://www.het-imo.net/project/the-mystery-of-leadership/

Covey, S. R. (1989). *The 7 habits of highly effective people*. New York, NY: Free Press.

Covey, S. R. (2004). *The 7 habits of highly effective people: Powerful lessons in personal change*. New York, NY: Free Press.

Eliot, T. S. (1943). *Little Gidding*. Little Gidding. Retrieved from http://www.columbia.edu/itc/history/winter/w3206/edit/tseliotlittlegidding.html

Jacobs, M., & Cooper, B. (2015). *Action research in the classroom: Helping teachers assess and improve their teaching*. Lanham, MD: Rowman & Littlefield.

Milton, J. (1667). *Paradise lost*. The Milton Reading Room. T. Luxon, Ed. Retrieved from https://www.dartmouth.edu/~milton/reading_room/pl/book_1/text.shtml

NIST/BPEP. (2016, September 21). Baldridge criteria 101. Baldridge Performance Excellence Program. Retrieved from https://www.nist.gov/baldrige/products-services/baldrige-excellence-builder

Passuello, L. (n.d.). Einstein's secret to amazing problem solving (and 10 specific ways you can use it). Litemind. Retrieved from https://litemind.com/problem-definition

Pólya, G. (1945). *How to solve it*. Princeton, NJ: Princeton University Press.

Weintraub, P. (2015, June 9). The voice of reason. *Psychology Today*. Retrieved from https://www.psychologytoday.com/articles/201505/the-voice-reason

Chapter 14

Whatever You Are, Be a Good One

Leadership and learning are indispensable to each other.

—John F. Kennedy

Personal mastery never ends; learning must continue into areas that do not even exist yet, including developments in brain research, useful and productive means of using technology, human development; and the future of education. Thinking about the future of leadership suggests that the learning leader is always moving forward in learning as well as leading. The teaching roles of leadership, generative leadership, the leader as learner and as the principal learner in any organization help leaders at all levels and in many roles contribute to the development of all learning leaders within and even beyond the organization.

The idea that personal mastery and learning about leadership is a never-ending journey suggests a trajectory for leadership. As with any journey, there is potential for learning along the way: potential, yes, because what can be learned is largely the choice of the traveler. This might be a first step on the journey of growing into leadership—to understand what impels a person to seek or accept a leadership responsibility. This chapter summarizes the path from personal mastery to organizational transformation

WHY THE DESIRE TO LEAD?

Whether holding a hierarchical position or sharing ideas about how to make things better without a position, there are some common reasons for wanting to be a leader: money, power, prestige. These can be potent impulses to take on a leadership position or leadership responsibility if called upon.

Paradoxically, Professor Seijts was surprised to learn that some of the leaders he interviewed for his book lacked an early, burning ambition to be glorified as a leader and some could not even recall when they joined the leadership ranks or made a conscious choice to be a leader. In an article for the *Ivey Business Journal*, Seijts (2013) goes on to report that what drove some was a desire to make a positive impact as an individual or team member. It was a formal leadership role that sparked a desire to excel as an organizational head but also reinforced the willingness to collaborate with and trust the judgment of others. That was a key lesson.

MONEY

Money, too, is a powerful motivator (Arnulf, 2014). However, it is debatable that money is the most powerful motivator to hold a leadership position. For those who have a mission, money can provide dignity for the family and a way to be altruistic. Money can also motivate for less noble reasons: because of the power that accompanies it, having the ability to operate without constraints, not having to be frugal, and being able to work in isolation without worrying about or even needing other people.

However, money is not the only, nor the prime, motivator. In fact, an earlier chapter pointed out that meaningful work and helpful relationships have greater motivational potential than money. Being able to learn on the job, being challenged to think outside the box is also a motivator. Being able to make a contribution and be recognized for it and helping others are motivators as well, which can be more powerful than money. Teamwork, a sense of belonging to something larger than oneself, the opportunity for generativity to help others grow can also be stronger motivators than money. Liking to go to work, having the opportunity to do what one loves and get paid for it has to be at the top of the list of powerful motivators (Foster, 2013).

VISION AND MISSION

Occasionally, someone will bring up the idea that choosing to work in nursing, teaching, counseling, advocating, or engaging social action is more than a job. Instead, it is a calling, a vocation. Henrietta's story of feeding the hungry was a good example. So was Denis's effort to found a school to be of service and advocate for the underserved. Lois started a school, raised the money for rent, does the advertising and marketing, meets parents, and sends her students off to Africa to dig wells. A job? Hardly!

What does that? What makes someone take the responsibility for and exercise the authority to start a school or a food kitchen, dig a well, go out on emergency calls? What makes others follow them and join them? Exemplars reveal the power of vision and mission. Dr. Ginger Grant (2014) is an innovation researcher whose article is a reminder of Joseph Campbell's (1968) description of such a calling as the hero's journey. Grant warned that answering the call, while it may be heroic, is not always pleasant. However, answering the call begins a transformational journey, first of oneself, and then of others' transformation, and then the transformation of the organization. Grant says, "the call formulates the beginning of the Core, the essence of the individual." The implication is that the essence is the vision and its facilitating mission. The more leaders know and learn about vision and mission, the better prepared they will be to invest time and energy in learning of others' missions and visions and the more clear the journey to transforming the organization will be.

TIME

Hildy Gottlieb (2007) believes that vision, mission, and values can change the world because they indicate where the organization is headed and what is needed to get there. However, Gottlieb also believes that it is the "rare organization that takes the time" to determine how to do the work to get there! In her view, time has a purpose and a product: Absent a values-based context for decision making, groups are more likely to default to fear-based decision making when things get tough. Those fear-based decisions are more likely to cross the very lines that the group agreed it would not cross, had they talked about those values before having to make a fear-based decision. The only defense against making regrettable fear-based decisions is to have discussed core values ahead of time.

DESIRE TO LEARN

Personal mastery requires a means to learn. It is quite possible that learning from research findings related to the brain may help with an understanding of developmental readiness for leadership. That is, understanding the neurological bases for transformational leadership behavior may make it possible to develop such leaders. Thus, instead of simply describing or promoting a one-size-fits-all concept of leadership development, learning more about the brain may give some insight into how effective leaders feel, think, and learn new behaviors.

Using such knowledge, leadership development might be customized based on the neurological structure of an individual leader whose actions seem effective. Such a conclusion, while it may seem paradoxical, does fit with Bennis's idea that leaders grow and develop from experience, and if effective leader behavior can be described it can be imitated. Neuroscience is at the beginning stages of describing how brains of effective leaders work. The leader who learns, desires to learn, and has the will to learn will want to know more about how to develop brain pathways to effectiveness.

Having interviewed thirty leaders from around the world, Professor Seijts (2013) gleaned lessons from lifetimes of leaders, the subtitle of his book that claims *good leaders learn*. He, too, was interested in the age-old question of whether leaders are born or made. What he found out was that leaders develop from "facing uncomfortable and difficult experiences." He claimed that his book project revealed that "good leaders develop through constant learning."

That learning included learning about themselves, their personalities, their relationships, and, ultimately, learning about the kind of leaders they wanted to become. Professor Seijts distilled ten pathways from what he learned from the leaders he interviewed. The pathways for learning to lead, having the desire to learn, and engaging their will to learn meant a journey from personal effort to the big picture of organizational transformation.

In summary, the pathways include performing and excelling in a role; risking or taking chances to lead and to learn; stretching by going beyond one's own personal comfort zone; learning, by taking the time to reflect on past events to discern the lessons offered; and self-awareness to deliberately seek to know one's personal strengths and weaknesses.

Also included in the pathways are trusting in and relying on one's abilities and those of others to build a reputation for being trustworthy; developing the ability to act appropriately in different situations; mentoring and learning from other leaders and role models on how to develop as a leader; observing and watching others and oneself to better understand events and situations; and finally, integrating and having the capacity to see and understand the *big picture*.

Professor Seijts calls it good news that "everyone I interviewed agrees that good leadership can be learned by anyone with basic smarts backed by an unwavering commitment to ongoing development and collaboration." The desire to learn is key.

SELF-TALK

Self-talk was considered in a previous chapter. This section reports self-talk in the form of letters that senior executives wrote to themselves that had a future orientation. The authors are from the Center for Creative Leadership, the University of North Carolina, and Northern Kentucky University (Rogelberg et al., 2013).

Their research examined leader self-talk via self-addressed future-oriented letters that executives wrote to themselves for their own personal development. As mentioned in the earlier chapter on self-talk, two types were revealed in the coding of the letters: positively related to effective leadership and creativity and dysfunctional self-talk that related negatively to effectiveness and creativity.

Rogelberg et al. (2013) provided evidence that leaders' free-flowing thoughts related to leaders' effectiveness and well-being and supported a self-leadership framework. Self-leadership was defined for their research as: "a comprehensive self-influence perspective that concerns leading oneself toward performance of naturally motivating tasks as well as managing oneself to do work that must be done, but is not naturally motivating" (p. 184).

> Leaders who are able to regulate their own emotions effectively through self-regulatory methods such as constructive self-talk should be better able to adapt to the needs of followers... Constructive self-talk allows a leader to reproduce the perspectives of other people more effectively and take these perspectives into account when making decisions. Here, self-talk provides the individual with an expanded frame of reference from which to view a problem, be it task or interpersonally focused, which is critical for effective problem solving. (p. 186)

PROBLEM SOLVING

Just as neuroscience is revealing the value of the leader's self-talk, there are also findings about the neuroscience of problem solving (Rock & Schwartz, 2006). The *strategy+business* website provided an article about using brain research findings to make organizational transformation a reality. The writers of the blog believe that managers who have some understanding of cognitive science can "lead and influence mindful change: organizational transformation."

The link from personal mastery to organizational transformation is in the form of applying learning about the physiological nature of the brain. Problem solving to achieve organizational transformation can be done only through the people who make up the organization. Participation can be affected by the past experience and memories of those who will undergo the solution—the change!

As a caveat, Rock and Schwartz mention six possible explanations that seem to discourage problem solving as a way to make change happen. These included the perception of change as painful and unexpectedly difficult because of physiological sensations provoked by organizational change as well as the fact that an effort to make changes to solve problems were not successful in the long run in spite of incentive and/or threat. Connection and persuasion did not seem to work either because of insufficient efforts to engage others.

The researchers also found several explanations that supported successful problem-solving activities. For example, repeated, purposeful, and attentive focus had power to influence personal development. The very act of paying attention caused chemical and physical change in the brain itself. Expectations also seemed to have an impact on how change was perceived and accepted.

POWER

Added to the list of motivators is the lure of power. Some view power as negative. Those for whom power is a negative may have in mind dictators and those who use their power to be cruel, overbearing, and hurtful. Power is associated with position, so workers think their bosses and the higher-ups have power. Sources of power vary, too. It comes from position, from expertise, from experience, from stature, and the like.

Schwartz and co-bloggers reported that neuroscientists and psychologists are beginning to learn what happens inside the mind and brain during mental activity. The leader who learns these dynamics and their effects may also learn more effective patterns of thinking and acting to choose those that benefit self and the organization. Doing so over time may make it possible to inspire others and help the organization reach and surpass its own goals.

Learning about power, its constructive use, and the importance of having power to get things done (the definition of leadership) means using power for effective personal behavior that may contribute to the effectiveness of the organization. The story that Schwartz and company tell about Natalie is instructive. The story has a happy ending and points to the teaching role of leadership that became possible through personal mastery, leading others to consider alternatives, and ultimately serving the organization.

The bloggers describe Natalie's (a pseudonym) situation when she was given some unpleasant responsibilities (including eliminating the jobs of thirty people) during a company downturn. These responsibilities caused Natalie stress and anxiety and contributed to her irritation at work. She feared losing her job. An executive coach helped Natalie begin a daily practice of focusing her attention on the reality behind her negative thinking. She eventually came to see her negative self-talk as messages from her brain that she could replace with more realistic—and therefore more positive—alternative thoughts.

Instead of continuing to focus on her own stress, Natalie began to learn how to think of strategies the company could use to improve its situation. With her newfound strategy, before attending meetings, Natalie talked to herself about how others might respond to her suggestions. She talked herself into making dispassionate comments rather than investing herself in them and suffering when they might not be accepted. Over time, she used her newly found power over her thoughts about her stressful situation to replace them with thoughts about how to help the company. As she gained opportunities to share these ideas, the power of her ideas became accepted, and she in turn became a partner who helped transform the organization (Schwartz, Thomson, & Kleiner, 2016). Hers became the teaching role of leadership.

PURPOSE

Natalie's power that strengthened her teaching role of leadership pointed to the power of purpose. The purpose of an organization is automatically future oriented. An accomplishment has to be planned and described before it even begins. The purpose has the power to create the future. The popularity of *The Purpose Driven Life* (Warren, 2012) and all the ancillary materials related to it reveal a strong desire for something worthwhile to hang one's life on. *The One Thing* (Keller & Papsan, 2012), the writings of the Dalai Lama, Parker Palmer's (2000) *Let Your Life Speak*, *The Secret* by Byrne (2006), and *The 7 Habits of Highly Effective People* talk of the power of creating the conditions that will produce in the future what is lacking in the present.

PEOPLE

If the job of the leader is to create leaders, then the leader has to practice all the aspects of leading self to help others lead themselves. The teaching role of leadership is future oriented. To lead others to lead themselves—short hand for developing leadership in others—requires believability. What gets said and what gets done must be congruent. If they are not, the trust level will diminish. If a leader is a boss, then boss language puts the burden of productivity on everyone else. The boss says "do this"! The leader says "please help, you are needed." When the work is done, bosses take the credit while leaders give credit.

The teaching role of leadership is essential when leading others to lead themselves. Leaders of the future will conduct themselves like experienced doctors in a teaching hospital. The resident physicians are given as much responsibility as possible for doing a doctor's work. They are supported by experts who are there to help. Leadership in the future will have a similar function. As much responsibility as possible must be given away without abdicating the responsibility for the outcome. They keep their employees informed and skip the mushroom theory of leadership—keep them in the dark and cover them with manure!

Dealing with people to create the organization of the future means the leader remains mindful of employees' needs for meaningful work. Consequently, future leaders give responsibility for appropriate critical experiences that provide challenge and learning on the job. At the same time, the leader supports, shares insight and know-how. The learning leader, who leads by learning knows how, is knowledgeable about the business, and uses technology appropriately. There is no bullying in the form of unilateral decision making because influential relationships have been built, nourished, and sustained.

Building the future of the organization is a group project. Independent thought is encouraged so it contributes to interdependent activity. Each person in the organization must be cognizant of stakeholder goals and purposes and must integrate those purposes into creating a culture of growth and initiative. Clear goals and purpose give power to leadership and engage followers. What is required is the permeation of purpose throughout the organization (Inam, 2013).

As seen earlier, a purpose changes a job to a calling or a vocation. A purpose that has the commitment of the members of an organization will engage the members deeply. The power of purpose operates like a touchstone. Similar to the work done by organizations to create their mission statements, the organizations of the future will verbalize their purpose and commit to measuring the impact of purpose on performance, productivity, and progress toward the realization of the vision.

Purpose forms the alpha and omega of the organization. It provides the impetus for organizational action. At the same time, accomplishing organizational purpose is a measure of the organization's legacy. The current efforts to create person-centered health care paves the way for future leaders to serve person-centered organizations. If future leaders at all levels of an organization choose a purpose of creating person-centered cultures, they will benefit from what Williams and Sanderson (2006) found to be the key elements for doing so.

Their list of key elements (in italics in following text) of person-centered leadership point to what leaders of the future must learn and practice. *Visionary leadership* will be the order of the day. Collective leadership will require *shared values and beliefs*. The person-centered organization of the future will require leaders to choose *outcomes for individuals* and a *community focus*.

An empowered and valued staff will be supported in their *individual learning* that contributes to *organizational learning*. *Partnerships* in the form of participantship will be the work of future leaders.

Developing future leaders will need to focus on the skills needed to promote participantship. Whether organizations will be able to resist the charismatic leader is debatable. Avoiding the negative aspects of the narcissism that often accompanies charismatic leadership will require a change in the criteria by which leaders are evaluated. Those criteria must include a disposition toward participantship, learning, and service to the mission.

Leaders of the future will also have to *hire up*, that is, hire people smarter than they are. Leaders will need those who use knowledge to serve the vision and mission with integrity and a disposition to be of use to others, whether internal and external to the organization. The respect for and value of those who work in the organization will require leaders of the future to be the thinkers, planners, designers, not micro managers. Future leaders will need to be mindful of the elliptical nature of the organization. The success of each individual must be integrated into the success of the company.

The leaders of the future will lead leaders not followers. Leading others to lead themselves is to lead leaders. The action that develops leaders is a hallmark of generative leadership. The commitment to the vision fuels the generativity of leading others to lead themselves. Connecting to other leaders in service to accomplishing the vision develops the strength and courage to live the mission.

Leadership of the future is the legacy of today's leadership. Those at all levels of leadership who want a part to play in creating the future need to take some steps to do so, to leave the legacy that will bear their imprint. Today's leaders will create the future by supporting those with the commitment and accountability for the vision. Positive self-talk needs to become standard operating procedure. It will need to be applied to problems, so that solutions are the result rather than complaints.

REFERENCES

Arnulf, J. K. (2014, November 13). *Money as a motivator. Business Review.* Retrieved from http://www.bi.edu/bizreview/articles/money-as-a-motivator/

Byrne, R. (2006). *The secret.* New York, NY: Atria Books.

Campbell, J. (1968). *The hero with a thousand faces.* 2nd Edition. Princeton, NJ: Princeton University Press.

Foster, J. (2013, August 23). *Is money the strongest motivator?* Wall Street Insanity. Retrieved from http://wallstreetinsanity.com/is-money-the-strongest-motivator/

Gottlieb, H. (2007). 3 statements that can change the world: Mission/vision/values. Help 4 NonProfits. Retrieved from http://www.help4nonprofits.com/NP_Bd_MissionVisionValues_Art.htm

Grant, G. (2014, August—November). Re-visioning the heroes journey: A story of something old, something new. *Integral Leadership Review*. Retrieved from http://integralleadershipreview.com/12278-1115-re-visioning-heroes-journey-story-something-old-something-new/

Inam, H. (2013, June 6). Why connecting to purpose makes us better leaders. Transformational Leadership. Retrieved from http://www.transformleaders.tv/why-connecting-to-purpose-makes-us-better-leaders/

Keller, G., & Papsan, J. (2012). *The one thing: The surprisingly simple truth behind extraordinary results*. Austin, TX: Bard Press.

Palmer, P. (2000). *Let your life speak: Listening for the voice of vocation*. New York, NY: Wiley and Sons.

Rock, D., & Schwartz, J. (2006, May 30). The neuroscience of leadership. Retrieved from strategy+business: http://www.strategy-business.com/article/06207?gko=6da0a

Rogelberg, S. G., Justice, L., Braddy, P. W., Paustian-Underdahl, S. C., Heggestad, E., Shanock, L., ... & Altman, D. G. (2013). The executive mind: Leader self-talk, effectiveness and strain. *Journal of Managerial Psychology*, 28(2), 183–201.

Schwartz, J., Thomson, J., & Kleiner, A. (2016, December 5). The neuroscience of strategic leadership. Retrieved from strategy+business: http://www.strategy-business.com/article/The-Neuroscience-of-Strategic-Leadership?gko=d196c

Seijts, G. (2013, July/August). Good leaders never stop learning. *Ivey Business Journal*. Retrieved from http://iveybusinessjournal.com/publication/good-leaders-never-stop-learning/

Warren, R. (2012). *Purpose driven life*. Grand Rapids, MI: Zondervan.

Williams, R., & Sanderson, H. (2006). *What we are learning about person centered organizations*. Retrieved at http://www.creativeoptionsregina.ca/wp-content/uploads/2015/03/What-are-We-Learning-About-Person-Centered-Organisations.pdf

Chapter 15

Participantship: The Future of Leadership

Leadership is not just about one person doing everything. Leadership is about lifting the team up. It's about making the collective better than the individuals. And it's about leaving the team better than it was before. Great leaders don't try and do everything forever, great leaders replace themselves.

—John Tornow

The signs of outstanding leadership appear primarily among the followers. Leading with others to transform the organization into more of what it is intended to be is the never-ending journey. It cannot be reached as a goal. The paradox of organizational transformation is the challenge to transform oneself.

The simple steps of leading self seem far from the organization. However, moving from dependence to independence is essential for the interdependence that exhibits itself in participantship, the hallmark of leadership. The ellipse as the metaphor for the organization highlights the two focal points of organizational effectiveness—the goals of the individual and the goals of the organization. Surrounded by the locus of points of stakeholders, the organization is in a constant state of kaizen—ever improving through the participation of members to meet global, social, and economic challenges. This chapter considers participantship and not merely followers as the future of leadership.

FOLLOW THE LEADER

Max Depree reminded us that the signs of outstanding leadership appear primarily among the followers. It sounds like the followers determine the leader. There is a cartoon showing someone running to catch up with a crowd of people running ahead. The caption reads: *I have to follow them! I am their leader!* It is a bit humorous but with a kernel of truth nonetheless. Leading *with* others becomes the moral imperative, to transform the organization into more of what it is intended to be. And the organization is made up of people, not only of spreadsheets or strategic plans!

From *super*man to all-in-together, the future of leadership is more collective, more centered in the participation that produces an authentic, honest, mission-driven organization. The signs of the future of leadership are already visible. Terms in use for some time preview a desired future for leadership; terms like *collective intelligence, lateral leadership,* and *integral leadership* add to the concepts of distributed leadership, total quality management, team leadership, and democratic leadership. The essence of participantship is in the collective nature of leadership that helps an organization thrive when all are invested.

FROM SUPERMAN TO ALL IN TOGETHER

Fullan and Hargreaves (2016) help us think about the components of moving from individual to collective development. Each component is on a continuum from the individual to the collective and includes autonomy, impact, responsibility, inquiry, efficacy, and mindset. It seems almost intuitive that leaders are at various places on the continuum at various times. However, tending toward collectivity in these areas can be seen as contributing to organizational transformation. While the individual aspect of the categories need not be seen as negative, increasing capacity to lead with others is required for organizational transformation.

The path to collectivity involves some basic understanding of the components. While individual autonomy represents the capacity to be one's own person without being manipulated or having reasons and motives distorted externally, collective autonomy represents the capacity to work collaboratively to acquire greater potential for development.

In an earlier article, Dr. Fullan (2014) provided several constructs for moving to collective autonomy: relentless high expectations that challenge the status quo, monitoring progress to take developmental action, transparency of results and practice, collective participation, purposeful collaboration, shared standards, using metrics and evidence regarding progress, engaging in processes that systematize the work, and an organization-wide commitment to be accountable to internal and external stakeholders. Moving to collective impact means to resist micro managing, focusing instead on actions that will shape the culture and develop the capacity of the group.

Leaders who shape an environment in which work is meaningful and accomplishes worthwhile goals also lead to organizational impact and transformation. Such an environment chooses a culture of *ours* over a culture of *mine* and also facilitates a sense of collective responsibility and collective efficacy.

Bandura (1986) described collective efficacy as the group's belief that it has the capability to attain its goals and accomplish the tasks needed to do so, that members' collective action could make a difference. Bandura proposed his theory to explain the social cognitive component of collective efficacy that he believed complemented and built on self-efficacy.

People do not live in social isolation, nor can they exercise individual control over various local situations or face all of life's challenges alone. Instead, shared problems require people to work together and to speak with a collective voice to improve their lives. The strength of families, communities, organizations, social institutions, or nations lies partly in people's sense of collective efficacy, the belief that they can solve the problems they face and improve their lives through unified effort.

If collective efficacy addresses issues of a social nature, then it follows that those who work together to effect a change must also serve each other by inquiring together, or at least inquiring for the group, to find sources of and solutions to the problem. The desire to learn will be beneficial if it is a group choice. Collective efficacy, the group's belief that problems can be solved, represents a positive mindset even in the face of difficult or negative conditions. In fact, John Hattie (2012) found teacher collective efficacy as the number one factor influencing student achievement, an example of collective efficacy in action.

THE BRAIN OF THE LEADER

The concepts of collective leadership are further enhanced by a deeper understanding of how the brain's 100 billion nerve cells are born, grow, and connect. Neuroscientists study brain cells to learn how they organize themselves into effective, functional circuits that usually remain in working order for life. Research in cognitive science seeks a greater understanding of personal and leadership behaviors and performance and focuses on neural patterns of leaders, brain agility and resilience, and, from an organizational standpoint, how to lead teams from a culture of fear to one of trust.

While not specifically identified as neuroscience, books like *Mindset*, *GRIT*, *The Organized Mind*, *Reclaim your Brain*, and *The One Thing* relate concepts of leading self to greater productivity, healthy relationships, and organizational effectiveness. In a variety of ways, these works apply neuroscience techniques to leadership development. Other works specifically related to neuroscience help individuals and teams examine leadership patterns, dealing with resistance to change and human emotions and cultivating creativity and cultural intelligence.

Leading self means recognizing the personal effects of findings from medical science and the cognitive psychology—that human capacity is affected by our brain waves, our chemistry, the thinking habits we have developed over time, attitudes we hold, to say nothing of the emotions that move us in certain directions. We, and those we work with, are changeable human beings living on a continuum from our best selves to our worst selves. The linear leader is not surprised, but patient, recognizing that there is no behavior beneath or beyond human beings.

IT IS NOT ABOUT LEADERSHIP AND IT IS NOT ABOUT FOLLOWERSHIP

The leadership that develops from participantship can be described as an expansion of the collective capacity of an organization's members to participate more effectively in leadership roles and processes (Day, 2001). This is the leadership that relies on growth-producing interactions, which uses deconstructive criticism, a strategy that carefully analyzes language in use to discover meaning and significance, to understand that what is being said from the speaker's point of view is just one of the possible interpretations. Kegan and Lahey's (2001) concept of deconstructive criticism in the workplace ameliorates a situation of well-intentioned but energy-dissipating constructive criticism.

Constructive criticism is a mismeme, based as it is on thinking that the person giving the constructive criticism usually is someone who holds a hierarchical position and has the correct view of a situation in need of improvement. The one with positional authority considers the comments as feedback. The employee or person receiving the feedback sees it as criticism, perhaps feeling that, since only a superior can give feedback, he or she may not offer a counter to it. Instead, collective leadership—participantship—shares the perceptions of the situation. Both—the giver and the receiver—share perceptions and understandings so that both are informed in the process.

WHAT HAPPENS IF THEY DON'T

Pat was working toward tenure as a high school teacher. Pat's supervisor, Lena, was placed in a supervisory position after only one year of experience doing workshops for high school students in need of assistance. Lena's only educational background was in literacy, and she based her observation on the degree she earned even though she had no experience with teaching. After observing a lesson on political satire using a Dr. Seuss story, Lena told Pat that the Seuss selection was way too basic for a class of high schoolers. "Your teaching is not geared to the class you have. You have to be more relevant to your group."

Stuck with this review, Pat just rolled her eyes at this revelation of illiteracy on Lena's part. However, because this was a case of the observer being the only one allowed to give feedback, Pat could only swallow hard. Calling attention to Lena's inability to understand the political undertones of Theodore Geisel's work would have made Lena adamant and defensive. As a result, there was no sharing of understanding or sharing of ways to improve the learning of the students. The general tone was "I'm right and you're wrong and don't you forget it": simply a lose-lose situation with the stakes much higher for Pat.

LATERAL LEADERSHIP

Nicky was asked to share her approach to teaching math to primary students with teachers from other schools. She was taken aback—"I'm just a teacher, I can't tell other people what to do." Frank was asked to lead a change initiative at the office that meant organizing his colleagues to gather needed data. He had no formal authority in his division, but he certainly wanted to succeed. Nicky and Frank, like so many who are asked to take on leadership without positions, were flattered but also anxious about how to get others to participate when they had no authority and nothing to offer by way of reward.

Enter the concept of lateral leadership. The superman or lone ranger approach—"I lead, you follow"—won't work. Instead, lateral leaders need skills rather than relying on the authority of a hierarchal position to engage their colleagues to work toward a goal as a team instead of a group that simply sits together in the same organization. The lateral leader has been working all along, networking, cultivating relationships, being a connector, and leading self. This preliminary work makes it possible for Nicky and Frank to persuade and negotiate, brainstorm and collaborate, create opportunities for participantship that focused on a goal to be reached.

A POSSIBLE FUTURE FOR LEADERSHIP

Lateral leadership is considered by some (Broderbauer, 2016) to be the leadership of the future. It means leadership without the power and authority that come from a hierarchical position. Not an entirely new concept, the seeds of lateral leadership are in distributive leadership, democratic leadership, and servant leadership. What is new about lateral leadership is the fact that it may be on a trajectory to becoming a more common approach to leadership.

In 2014, Rob Jacobs (2014) blogged about the CEO versus catalytic leadership, in which he commented on what may be a reason that lateral thinking is not the norm: catalysts rock the boat and are much better agents of change than those who protect the status quo. Catalysts (of lateral leadership, perhaps) are better accepted in extreme situations that might call for something radical that requires creative thinking.

A BOSS OR A LEADER?

Jacobs's comparison of the CEO and catalyst parallels that of the conventional leader and lateral leader. The CEO is a boss who uses command and control, insists on ignoring values and feelings in favor of the rational, and uses and abuses the power of position to make things happen. Conventional CEOs are directive, seek the spotlight, and want order imposed by decision making, as though before they arrived nothing had been done in the organization. CEO language includes "didn't you hear what I said?" Why did you do that?" and "You should know better."

The catalyst on the other hand considers others to be peers, trusts them, and recognizes emotions and emotional intelligence as resources. Catalysts are inspired themselves by possibilities and can in turn be inspirational. They certainly are collaborative; they operate behind the scenes, giving others the opportunity to take center stage. Because they are willing to start in the middle and work toward the beginning and the end, there may be some ambiguity. While they connect the work, they also connect with others. They ask "what if," "why not," and "what do you think."

Conventional leadership holds sway in so many organizations that the concept that leadership exists at all levels of an organization is unusual and even threatening to those with a position. Regrettably, those with hierarchical positions may not even have leadership skill, so their anxiety is understandable when asked to recognize leadership among those without a position. The belief that there is leadership at all levels of an organization, with or without a position, is a threat to the conventional CEO, and, at the same time, the underpinning of lateral leadership.

Lateral leadership means inviting, not telling, asking for ideas to design the process to reach a goal. This lateral leader is aware of and cares about the potential substantial effect of decisions on some members. That awareness and care about individuals and the organization will manifest itself in presenting the initiative as worthy of buy-in through a process of deconstructing the initiative and moving from concern or even conflict to consensus, with those most affected by the change. The lateral leader can grow and develop. What is required is understanding how lateral leadership differs from conventional leadership.

COMPARISON OF CONVENTIONAL AND LATERAL LEADERSHIP

A conventional leader thinks in terms of an action to be completed so there is an outcome or a decision, regardless of a win-lose result. The conventional leader leads by telling, requiring, directing. The conventional leader makes sure everyone knows who is in charge, even if not doing any of the work, just monitoring, micro managing, and insisting on "my way or the highway."

The lateral leader, on the other hand, works at the thinking component of the activity. Are there ideas that haven't been heard yet? Can anyone think of another way? The lateral leader asks, appreciates, and encourages divergent thinking. The lateral leader is exactly that—lateral—on the side, letting others take the credit, as Depree recommends.

Conventional leaders operate in conventional ways, predictably, like bosses intent on pleasing higher-ups. They often give orders that come from higher-ups or present orders as coming from higher-ups. They deal with issues one at a time, separate from each other, not part of a cohesive whole of continuous improvement. They seek to fix one thing effectively and efficiently, often with a view to impressing higher-ups by focusing on the minute and the particular, with no vision or view of the whole, no strategies related to future improvement. Staff and employees and directors are all subordinates, even those who are department or division heads responsible for other employees. All have to be watched and prodded: theory X in action!

Lateral leaders have an opposite viewpoint. They believe in collective intelligence and that all of us is smarter than one of us. They want to know if there are new methods or new ways of thinking about the issue. Lateral leaders question the process and the approach and encourage others to use their talents and abilities. Their focus is on what can be on how a current issue will mean a better organization down the line. They ask, they don't tell, they delegate, and they look for and create opportunities for participantship.

Conventional leaders pride themselves on being decisive, which they are without consultation. They engage in unilateral decision making (a form of bullying!), select favorites to take over, and give the CEO's orders: "execute and implement them." The focus is on action and short-term results without giving thought to integration and the needs of the organization. They discourage dissent and can be vindictive about it. Their want is to promote self and act out of self-interest. They praise and seek dependence, confusing it for cooperation. Conventional leaders overrule others' ideas and initiatives, claiming them to be wrong, unnecessary, and extraneous.

If an idea is presented with which they are unfamiliar, they consider it to be nonexistent, especially when they themselves lack knowledge of other possibilities. They fabricate easily to look good or to seem knowledgeable. Conventional leadership is defensive, manages by memo and email, and claims legitimacy by reference to higher-ups.

Once again, lateral leaders operate differently: they look for differences, appreciate perceptions outside of group think. They focus on the end product by encouraging a variety of ways to get to it. They look for partners when hiring, those who will bring creativity, experience, talent, capability, and the independence needed for authentic interdependence. Lateral leaders listen for ideas on the fringes and for analytical and intuitive approaches to problem solving. Individual initiative is highly regarded and encouraged to try the not yet proven. They communicate constantly, individually and collegially.

The lateral leader's goal is a better organization. The decision-making process occurs and progresses with colleagues and employees, the internal customers. Lateral leaders look for leaders everywhere in the organization. If they are leaders with hierarchical positions, lateral leaders recognize the need to help develop leadership, especially among those who are not formally or officially in charge.

What are the chances that there will be a paradigm shift that will recognize the education, training, expertise, leadership of everyone in the organization? Or will leadership continue to be recognized by position rather than by talent? Based on some of the sad stories of what happens if they don't, a shift is certainly needed. The world has changed, and technology has made collective intelligence a realizable construct.

INTEGRAL LEADERSHIP

Believing that conventional leadership is fundamentally flawed, integral leadership is presented as a "half-step" (Forman & Ross, 2013) toward a solution. The authors quote Thomas Friedman in their introduction about dealing with the crisis in conventional leadership: "We are either going to rise to the level of leadership, innovation, and collaboration that is required, or everybody is going to lose—big. Just coasting along and doing the same old thing is no[t] an option any longer. We need a whole new approach" (p. 2).

That approach is conceived by the authors as integral leadership. The authors are not alone. There are sites dedicated to the idea of changing the way business operates. Management Innovation eXchange (Alcide, Raphael, Passarella, & Almeida, 2012), for example, invites participants to consider and suggest large ideas that focus management on higher purposes, rethink the philosophical foundations, and redefine the work of leadership.

Integral leadership invites ideas—hacks—to "help invent the future of management" by suggesting any idea for fixing "big, thorny challenges . . . [with] big unconventional ideas." The site invites ideas as basic as suggesting a way to run meetings or a large goal of overhauling compensation. The aim is to unearth an idea that "turns the tables on management-as-usual" and "points to a way to promote one of the large purposes" (Alcide, Raphael, Passarella, & Almeida, 2012).

One of the contributors to the site is Daniel Pink, author of *Drive: The Surprising Truth About What Motivates Us*. In a short video, Pink describes the flawed thinking of conventional management about individual motivation. Pink wants to reform that flawed thinking to help people soar. Integral leadership is designed to allow leadership at all levels of the organization to flourish, instead of being quashed. Because of the entrenched mode of operating by conventional leaders and organizations, encouraging integral leadership seems an almost combative activity.

What is required is "beholding the universe [the organization?] through the eyes of another [of a colleague? an employee?], of a hundred others [the stakeholders of the organization?], to behold the hundred universes that each of them beholds, that each of them is" (with apologies to Proust, 2010).

It is unlikely that someone in a hierarchical position in a conventional organization will be able to "behold the universe through the eyes of another" as a function of leadership. On the other hand, it is exactly what the integral leader seeks—to see leadership in a hundred others at whatever evolutionary stage of leadership they may be. The integral leader has the best chance to influence an environment conducive to ongoing leadership development and growth that has opportunities for participantship. Integral leaders use personal leadership behavior to contribute to organizational and cultural transformation. Shared values permeate all systems and processes through behavior and performance, not position.

A POSITION OR A PERFORMANCE

Conventional leaders in conventional organizations hold positions, perhaps one they had to compete for. As a result of securing a position, conventional leaders need only perform the tasks that got them the job. But, linear leadership, integral leadership, collective leadership require action, not position. Performance is easily understood in an athlete, not so much in a leader.

Some athletes train daily, some for hours. They devote 90 percent of their time to training to improve their performance by 10 percent. Leaders barely think of training. However, leading self to act on a vision or mission requires practice, reflection, and trying again. Using time to create a product requires discipline and repeated performance to develop effective time management as a habit.

Self-talk, that powerful strategy for good or ill, is tenacious in its negativity. Developing an abundance (positive) mentality requires serious and untiring efforts to replace a scarcity mentality. Desiring to learn, even at the top of the hierarchy, means carving out time to learn, maintaining a curiosity of mind, developing self-efficacy that such an investment in oneself has a payoff. Holding a problem-solving stance means seeing problems as opportunities. Unending deliberate practice develops a disposition toward a problem-solving frame of mind.

LEADING TO TRANSFORM

Having considered personal mastery, leading others to lead themselves, and leading with others to transform the organization, the groundwork has been laid for future leadership. Leading others so they lead themselves is an investment in the future. The learning leader is the leader of the future. Today's is a knowledge society. There is no end to how much knowledge will be generated. Thought leaders are the leaders of the future. Culturally intelligent leaders will continue to transform organizations in the future. Design thinking will characterize the leaders of tomorrow.

Leaders will continue to drive success as they set goals and monitor results, scan the external environment, define vision and strategy, design (consciously or by default) the infrastructure of the organization, develop people and build culture. Tomorrow's leaders will take seriously the dictum to challenge the process, their own mental models and comfortable assumptions, and traditional roles and practices.

For these leaders, such a challenge will no longer be an innovation. Rather, it will be the mode of operating that uses the collective knowledge and intelligence of leaders at all levels in the organization. Collaboration will no longer be the hallmark of extraordinary companies but the ordinary hallmark of their organizations. They will expect, support, and sustain agility, flexibility, responsiveness. There will be no longer a need to require compliance. Commitment to the vision and mission will make compliance unnecessary. Commitment will drive individual and group action, belief and behavior.

There will be boldness born of freedom from fear of mistakes and incurring displeasure. Position will determine responsibility and accountability. The transformed organization's mantra will be these words attributed to Goethe: *Whatever you can do or dream you can, begin it! Boldness has genius, power, and magic in it.*

REFERENCES

Alcide, R., Raphael, R. A., Passarella, W., & Almeida, F. (2012, May 11). It's time to reinvent management. Management Innovation eXchange. Retrieved from http://www.managementexchange.com/hack/integral-leadership-%E2%80%93-comprehensive-approach-developing-leaders-who-can-promote-fundamental-ren

Bandura, A. (1986). *Social foundations of thought and action: A social cognitive theory*. Englewood Cliffs, NJ: Prentice-Hall.

Broderbauer, J. (2016, May 11). Why do we need a new leadership approach? MDI Blog. Retrieved from https://www.mdi-training.com/blog/blog/new-leadership-approach/

Day, D. D. (2001). Leadership development: A review in context. *The Leadership Quarterly* 11(4), 581–613.

Forman, J. P., & Ross, L. A. (2013). *Integral leadedrship: The next half-step*. Albany, NY: State University of New York Press.

Fullan, M. (2014, Spring). Leadership: Maximizing impact. Retrieved from http://michaelfullan.ca/wp-content/uploads/2016/06/14_Spring_Maximizing-Impact-Handout.compressed.pdf

Fullan, M., & Hargreaves, A. (2016, December 5). Professional learning and development. Learning Forward Annual Conference 2016. Retrieved from http://michaelfullan.ca/wp-content/uploads/2016/12/16_Fullan_Hargreaves_Learning-Forward-2.key.pdf

Hattie, J. (2012). *Visible learning for teachers*. New York, NY: Routledge.

Jacobs, R. (2014, January 28). CEO vs. catalytic leadership. "Cross"-Pollination. Retrieved from http://robjacobs.tv/ceo-vs-catalytic-leadership/

Kegan, R., & Lahey, L. L. (2001). *How the way we talk can change the way we work: The seven languages for transformation*. San Francisco, CA: Jossey-Bass.

Proust, M. (2010). *In search of lost time, Vol 5: The captive & the fugitive*. New York, NY: Random House.

Index

authority, 10, 14, 19, 21, 24, 25, 27, 29, 115, 116, 135, 138, 159, 170–72

Bass, Bernard, 6, 26
behavior, 4, 9–10, 14, 16, 18, 21, 27, 33, 36, 40, 43, 51, 61, 66, 76, 77–78, 79, 80–81, 82, 85, 88, 90, 93, 94, 107, 109, 110, 125–26, 129, 136, 138–39, 149, 159–60, 162, 169–70, 175, 176; RISC to change, 16, 66, 88–89; structure influences, 116–18
Bennis, Warren, 3, 160
Burns, James MacGregor, 3, 6, 109, 111

change, 6, 14, 16, 18, 19, 21, 23, 25, 29, 35, 40, 42, 49, 54, 59, 68, 76, 85, 90–94, 97–101, 107, 109, 118, 121, 123–30, 133, 135, 137, 139, 147–48, 15691, 161–62, 164–65, 169–75. *See also* behavior; conflict
commitment, 10–11, 15, 17, 19–20, 29, 38, 43, 47, 50, 53, 86, 98, 109–10, 112, 117–18, 127, 131, 149, 160, 164–65, 168, 176
communication, 7, 17–18, 28, 37, 56, 78, 80–81, 85–88, 95, 97, 99–103, 107, 117, 138, 149
complaint, 56, 98–100, 165

compliance, 11, 25, 82, 95, 109–10, 117, 176
conflict, 5, 11, 16, 18, 45, 73, 74, 76, 78–81, 82, 85, 89, 93, 94, 100, 109, 112, 117, 125, 130, 173
connectedness, 16, 21, 112, 115, 133, 136–42
consensus, 45, 73, 76, 81, 85, 92, 105, 137, 142, 173
contingency theory, 4, 6
Covey, Stephen, 28, 35, 36, 46–48, 50, 51, 59, 107, 112, 135, 149, 151–52
culture, 10, 15, 19–20, 76, 90, 93, 95, 100, 107, 111, 116, 117, 118, 125, 129, 133, 134, 140, 142, 149, 150, 164, 168–69, 176

decision-making, 89, 126, 152, 174
dependence, vii, 11, 20, 29, 97, 104, 110, 121, 136, 167, 170, 174. *See also* independence; interdependence
DePree, Max, 74, 82–83, 85, 167, 173
design, 18, 85, 89, 94, 100, 110–11, 134–36, 176
dignity, 6, 11, 14, 16, 21, 112, 118, 135–39, 158
dispositions, 10–11, 14, 59–60, 62–64, 67–69, 94, 98, 100, 107, 133–34, 139, 151–52, 165, 176

Dorfman, H. A., 40, 60
Drucker, Peter, 13, 36, 100
Duhigg, Charles, 38, 77, 91, 93, 103

efficacy, 141, 168; collective, 155, 169; self, 53, 176
effectiveness, 5, 52, 112, 117, 137, 139, 148, 154, 160–62, 167, 169
employees, 76, 118, 134–36, 170, 175
empower, 47, 101; empowerment, 7, 90
excellence, 11, 14–16, 21, 47–48, 93, 115, 129, 135, 137–39, 148

feedback, 18, 64, 73, 75–76, 81, 88, 101, 105, 111, 117, 128, 130, 138, 148, 170, 171
Fiedler, Fred, 4–6
future, viii, 17–18, 20–21, 26, 28–29, 35, 38, 42, 46–47, 61, 110–11, 115, 125, 133, 135, 137–42, 157, 161, 163–67, 168, 172–73; of leadership, 145–55, 173–76. *See also* participantship

goals, 6, 10, 14, 16, 25, 28, 36, 38–40, 43, 47, 49–51, 76, 79–81, 86, 103, 109–11, 114–16, 130, 134, 149, 162, 164, 167, 169, 176
groups, 4–5, 16, 18, 23, 26, 34, 38, 48, 54, 60, 75, 80–81, 89, 94, 98, 101, 103, 107, 111–12, 116–17, 130, 141, 152, 155, 159, 164, 168–69, 171, 174, 176
growth, 16–18, 21, 25, 36, 38, 59, 68, 81, 93, 96, 129–30, 138, 149, 152, 164, 175; growth-producing2, 11, 85, 96, 109–10, 136, 170

habit, 16, 36, 39, 47, 53, 77–78, 80, 82, 93–94, 97–98, 101, 112, 170, 176
hiring, 95, 124, 126, 128, 174

ideas, 4, 6, 10, 17, 24–26, 28, 39, 47, 49, 62–63, 76, 82, 86, 89, 94, 102, 111–12, 116, 123, 126, 130, 135, 137, 140–41, 157–58, 160, 163, 173–75
independence, vii, 11, 20, 29, 60, 121, 167, 170, 174. *See also* dependence; interdependence
individual, vii, 10, 14, 20, 23, 34, 43, 53–54, 62, 64–66, 75, 79–81, 90, 95, 98, 104, 107, 109, 111–12, 114–18, 123, 127, 130, 134–36, 138, 148, 158–61, 165, 167–70, 173–76
interactions. *See* growth-producing3
interdependence, vii, 11, 20, 29, 121, 127, 167, 170, 174. *See also* dependence; independence
integral. *See* leadership: integral

Jones, Laurie Beth, 35, 46, 48
justice, 48, 82, 117, 125

kaizen, 10, 52, 150, 167
Kissinger, Henry, 23, 25
knowledge, skills, dispositions, vii–viii, 10–11, 13–14, 16–21, 29, 31, 33, 37–38, 59, 62, 73, 75, 82, 85, 93, 138–39, 150

LEADER process, 153–55
leaders: immigrant, 15–19, 59; traits, 3–7, 24, 63, 76
leadership: behavior, 4, 9–10, 14, 16, 18, 21, 27, 33, 36, 40, 43, 51, 61, 66, 76–82, 85, 88, 90, 93–94, 107, 109–10, 116–18, 125–26, 129, 136, 138–39, 149, 159–60, 162, 169–70, 175–76; characteristics, vii, 3, 4, 7–9, 17, 63, 76, 110, 112, 148, 151; collective, viii, 20, 38, 90, 123, 145, 148, 164, 167–76; entrepreneurial, 9, 15, 138–39; integral, 116, 145, 168, 174–76; lateral, 145, 168, 171–74; linear, 154, 170, 175; mismeme, 17, 76, 134, 170; myths, 9–11; style, 5–6, 16, 101; teaching role of, 18, 91, 135, 138, 152, 157, 162–63; theories, 4, 6–7, 14, 21,

41, 79, 109–10, 137, 164, 169, 173; transformational, 6–7, 26, 29, 47, 109, 159
leading: self vii, 31–61; others, vii, 1, 10, 16–17, 29, 71–105, 154, 163. *See also* organizational transformation; self-talk
learning organization, 15, 125, 135, 137, 148, 150. *See also* organizational learning
legacy, 16, 20, 82, 135, 137–38, 164–65
Lencioni, P., 75, 89, 90
Llopis, Glenn, 15, 19
love, 67, 75, 82, 134–35

management, 4, 14, 28, 53, 56, 80, 86, 92, 94, 116, 137, 139, 148, 150, 168, 175
Manz, C. C., 40, 53–54, 102, 135, 161
mastery, vii, 13, 15–17, 29, 31, 45, 65–66, 102, 138, 149, 151–52, 157, 159, 161
McGuire, J. B., 19–20
mission, vii, viii, 9–11, 14, 16, 18, 20, 25, 26, 28–29, 31, 33, 35–36, 38, 40, 43, 45–46, 47–48, 49, 62, 74, 75, 80, 86, 104, 107, 110, 115–16, 118, 131, 133, 137, 138–39, 141, 142, 147, 148, 149, 150, 158–59, 164–65, 168, 176
motivation, 6, 18, 40, 51, 73, 76–77, 79, 94, 95, 109, 158, 175
Mulford, Prentice, 62, 68

organizational: effectiveness, 137, 167, 177; learning, 21, 133, 165; transformation, vii–viii, 28, 107, 110, 136, 139–40, 147, 150, 157, 161, 167, 168, 170
organizations, vii–viii, 4, 7, 13, 19, 28, 33, 46, 62, 68, 75, 78–79, 95, 103, 109–10, 112, 117, 134–35, 137–39, 141, 148, 150, 164–65, 169, 172, 175–76; as an ellipse, 112–16

participantship, viii, 23, 25, 90, 109–11, 121, 133, 140, 148, 165, 167–71, 173, 175
practice, deliberate, 14, 127–30, 176
problem-solving, 10, 33, 54, 94, 125, 128, 148, 152–54, 176
productivity, 20, 36, 42, 52, 66, 93, 95, 134, 150, 163–64, 169

relationship-oriented. *See* Fiedler, Fred
RISC. *See* behavior

self-talk, vii, 10, 12, 16, 18, 20, 28–29, 31, 33, 39–40, 43, 45, 52–54, 59, 65–66, 69, 78, 85, 86, 105, 110, 143, 148, 150–51, 152, 154, 155, 160–61, 162, 165, 176
Senge, Peter, 17, 48, 65, 129, 134–35, 138, 152
skill, 3, 10, 37–38, 45, 48–49, 53, 55, 59, 63, 75, 79, 82, 85–86, 93–94, 98, 102, 111, 121, 127–28, 130, 133, 139, 148–49, 154
Smith, Glenn, 28–29
stakeholders, 21, 28, 103, 111, 121, 127, 134–39, 141, 148, 164, 168–69, 175
strategy, 29, 56, 80, 112, 154, 161, 163, 166, 170, 176, 184
structure, 5, 13–14, 21, 77, 109–10, 116–19, 143, 160, 176
success, 8, 15, 20, 24, 35–36, 39, 49, 51–54, 61–63, 69, 83, 93, 100, 103, 110, 117, 121, 126–27, 129, 135–36, 139, 151–52, 155, 162, 165, 176; successful failure, 26–29, 74, 105
supervision, 18, 34, 64, 88, 97, 102–3, 130, 134, 171
synergy, 20, 75, 127

talent, 1, 9, 18, 52, 89–90, 102, 111, 115, 126–30, 140, 143, 173–74
task-oriented. *See* Fiedler, Fred
teams, 18, 75, 83, 85, 89–90, 92, 95, 103, 105, 116–18, 169–70; team members, 77, 89–90, 103, 117, 149, 153; teaming, 74–75, 85, 90, 95, 115

time management, 14, 37, 51, 69, 105, 143, 148–49, 176; 168 hours, 45, 48–49, 69, 134; use of time, 33, 36, 49, 141, 150

Tracy, Brian, 36, 38, 41, 43, 51

transformational leadership, 5, 6, 26, 47, 109, 139, 159

trust, 5, 17, 76, 83, 87, 89, 97, 99–100, 103, 110, 134, 158, 160, 163, 169, 172; level of, 99, 163

values, 11, 15–16, 28, 36, 45–48, 79–81, 103, 112, 125, 137–38, 159, 164, 172, 175

Vanderkam, Laura, 49. *See also* time management: 168 hours

vision, vii, 1, 13, 15, 17, 19–20, 26–29, 31, 33–38, 42, 45–47, 49, 56–57, 60, 65, 67, 75, 86, 91, 95, 107–8, 130, 133–35, 139, 142, 148, 173, 176; and mission, 9–11, 25, 28, 31, 33, 43, 45, 46, 110, 118, 131, 137, 141, 148–50, 159, 165, 176; visionary, 62, 135, 164

will to act, 10, 29, 77

will to learn, vii, 9–10, 28–29, 45, 135, 141, 148, 150, 152–54, 160

Contributors

Sister Mary Ann Jacobs, scc, EdD, is adjunct Associate Professor of School Building Leadership in the Graduate Education Program at Manhattan College in Riverdale, New York. She has served in several leadership capacities: classroom teacher, principal, associate superintendent, professor, principal investigator for an NSF grant. She prepares future leaders in education. Her research interests include STEM education, action research, brain-compatible instruction, and effective middle schools.

Sister Remigia Kushner, csj, PhD, is Professor of Education and Director of Educational Leadership in the Graduate Education Program at Manhattan College. Dr. Kushner has been an elementary and secondary school teacher of math and science, a secondary principal, a district and associate superintendent with responsibility for the recruitment, retention, and development of school leaders. Her research interests include professional development, continuous improvement of teaching and learning, and reflective leadership practice.

www.ingramcontent.com/pod-product-compliance
Lightning Source LLC
Chambersburg PA
CBHW030112010526
44116CB00005B/213